# The Promise of a Sound Mind

God's plan for emotional and mental health

Eddie Snipes

## A book by:
## Exchanged Life Discipleship

I0157349

Published by GES Book Publishing
Carrollton, GA

Copyright © 2012 by Eddie Snipes, Exchanged Life
Discipleship, and GES Book Publishing

http://www.exchangedlife.com

ISBN: 978-0-9832247-5-4
Revision A

Contact the author by visiting
http://www.eddiesnipes.com or
http://www.exchangedlife.com

# Table of Contents

# Introducing the Sound Mind

Life is more than chasing after feelings. Our emotional health and feelings of happiness are by-products of a healthy lifestyle and attitude. A life built upon a dependence on any emotion is destined for frustration and heartache.

This book is a tool which is intended to guide you toward establishing the foundation of your life on solid ground, and from this firm foundation, healthy emotions can flourish. If you approach life from the perspective of trying to fill the void within by pursuing happiness, decision making will be flawed, and your reactions will lack good rationale. You will be tempted to leave behind what is healthy in order to pursue what you think will create happiness.

Happiness is a temporary feeling. If it is the focus of life, joy will be absent. Joy comes by focusing on the things which have lasting value, but the pursuit of happiness focuses on what is only for the moment. Pleasures and things may make us happy for a moment, but when the moment has passed, the object of our focus is lost. We'll then try to fill the void of emptiness by again searching for the first thing we think will make us happy. Or we'll lash out at anyone who threatens our fragile happiness.

Consider the wise words of Proverbs 16:3, "Commit your works to the LORD and your thoughts will be established." To be established is the beginning of true joy. Joy is the satisfaction of knowing something good is before us that we know will satisfy. It can be both a distant hope and a present assurance. The joy of the Lord is our strength; therefore, to be established on His secure foundation directly affects how we view and approach life.

A house is no stronger than its foundation. A home built on a failing foundation will break down quickly. The home owner must constantly be vigilant to make repairs in order to keep the house from falling into decay, or if the foundation is bad enough, from collapsing. Some structures, when the damage is too severe, are abandoned. It's often easier to give up than to fix the damage.

Life is no different. A strong life cannot be built upon a damaged foundation. The foundation must be repaired first, and then the symptoms can be addressed. What we assume is the problem in our lives is instead one of the symptoms of a flawed foundation.

The truth is we are all standing on a flawed foundation from birth. Out of the womb, our focus is to feed ourselves, fulfill our desires, and to obtain the things we think will make us happy. That is the foundation every life is built upon, and it's flawed. Some people learn to cope in different ways. Some learn to compromise with others. Some learn to hide their pain and put on a happy face. Regardless of our outward presentation, each one of us needs a foundation that is greater than the drive to fulfill self-centered motives.

Crying to be fed, held, and given material things may be something that works for infants, but it doesn't last and certainly can't be the foundation of a satisfying adulthood.

This book is unapologetically Christian. However, even Christians struggle with the concept of living for a purpose that is greater than getting immediate gratification. The truth is until we learn what it means to have intimacy with God, we cannot fully grasp the joy of living a fulfilled life.

In my book, _Simple Faith: How every person can experience intimacy with God_, I go into the foundations of the Christian life and what it means to know God. Like this book, I've made _Simple Faith_ available for a dollar. If you can't afford this, email me through my website and I'll get you an e-book copy for free.

While this book focuses on the emotional structure of our lives, Simple faith focuses on the Spiritual foundation of our lives. Without a good foundation, we will get discouraged, for the emotional cracks will be spreading faster than we can repair them.

The reality of life is that you cannot repair the foundation you are built upon. But God has promised to take your old life, bury it, and give you a new life which is born in Christ, and give you a new spirit which is incorruptible and able to overcome anything in the world. This new life rests on the sure foundation of Christ, and it becomes the house which does not fall – even when beaten by the storms of life.

With this understanding, let us now examine God's promise of a sound mind.

Come with me on a journey of discovery. One thing I've learned through a decade and a half of ministry is this: True discipleship / mentoring / advice is not me telling you what to think or do. True discipleship comes from the heart. It is my journey of discovery.

True Christian discipleship is not a guru telling followers what to think or do. It is someone responding to God's call to share their life with others. A discipler is a disciple who is sharing what they are learning as they walk where God leads, and then teaching others what they also are learning. It's a partnership of growth between two or more people. The teacher is not greater than the disciple; he or she is merely sharing what God is teaching them with others, so they too can learn how to walk with God on a deeper level.

I'm sharing with you the things I am learning and striving to overcome. We are all on a journey and each of us has pitfalls and victories. I'm here to share what the Lord is revealing in me, and I'm inviting you to come along with me on this portion of my pilgrimage toward eternity. My hope is you will get a glimpse of some of the things I'm discovering and draw out what applies to your life.

The truths I'm about to share have been life-changing for me. These biblical principles have shaped my life in the past, are changing me as I write, and continue to give me hope and encouragement for the future. These truths are especially encouraging when facing struggles and life's hardships.

One thing I have learned while writing this book is how easy it is to let truths slip from my focus. Things I should live by begin to slide into the back of my mind, and I forget to apply what I know to my daily life. Writing this book has reminded me of many things I also need to live by, and it has been good for me to be reminded. I encourage you to find a way to apply these truths to your life, and ways to keep them in constant remembrance. Otherwise you will read and forget, but not profit from the promises of God which are given when we keep His instructions.

You may have heard the statement, "Knowledge is power." When it comes to biblical truth, knowledge isn't power. Knowledge is the instruction which leads us to God's power. Knowing truth doesn't profit us until we surrender ourselves to it. The Bible gives us knowledge of God's ways, but until we apply it by faith, it is merely words on the pages of scripture.

In Old Testament times, when God's people knew truth but failed to act on it, the people missed out on the promises of God. Or as the book of Hebrews states, "The word didn't profit them, not being mixed with faith."[1]

Faith is a gift of God. It is God presenting His word to us, opening our eyes to see its truths, and then calling for us to submit our lives to His ways. Until we put it into practice, knowing truth does not profit us. Sometimes we have to step into what we can't see while believing what God has said is true.

I'm learning this the hard way. Many times I have been unwilling to let go of my control, and therefore have lived under many unnecessary burdens. Yet when I have the faith to believe God and trust Him, I discover the amazing life He breathes into my spirit. My prayer is you will begin experiencing this in your own life as well. The greatness of God's grace is that He doesn't reach into our lives because

---

[1] Hebrews 4:2

we are worthy, but because He is good. He delights in transforming broken lives and unworthy people into trophies of His glory.

The truths from scripture discussed throughout this book can change your life. They are easy to understand, but difficult to live by. Difficult because it requires us to let go of what our human nature clings to. Human nature will hold onto destructive behaviors and attitudes rather than submitting to the truth and surrendering control to the Lord. Even when our ways aren't working, we naturally resist God's ways because they are contrary to human nature.

It isn't knowing truth that changes your life. It is living in truth that changes your life. Knowledge comes first, but it doesn't profit anyone without faith. Knowledge of God's life-changing principles are necessary in order to release what is harmful and grasp what is empowering. Then you have to believe and give yourself to God's work in your life.

The Lord is already reaching out to you.

His goal is not to force you into submission, but to reach out with the hand of grace and call you to submit to Him. Until there is submission, Jesus isn't Lord of our hearts. Where Christ is Lord, the individual is lifted up. Where the individual is lord, that person is incomplete and limited to only what the flesh can grasp. Becoming our own lord is to forfeit what is eternal to grasp that which is dying and destined to decay.

There are few guarantees in life, but one thing which can be guaranteed is this. If you give yourself wholeheartedly to these biblical principles, meditate on them, and put them into practice, your life-changing progress will be evident to all (See 1 Timothy 4:15).

This is God's promise to you. It won't be easy, but if you apply your life to submitting to the instructions of God, the strength of the flesh (which includes your emotional flaws) will lose its grip, and those around you will see your life changing before their eyes. The promise is not that your life will merely improve in some areas, but that this change will be plainly evident to all. Your life will change – and dramatically. It's a promise for any who will apply their hearts to God's wisdom.

One temptation we all face is apathy. Even when motivated, it's easy to slip back into apathy and allow our human nature to rule us. This is why knowing truth is not enough. We must pursue it and then keep pursuing.

Don't settle for the lie that you're just wired the way you are. We are all wired with deficiencies. It's called the flesh – that which was born into a fallen human nature. Regardless of how defective your flesh is, the spirit of life within you has the God-ordained power to overcome any weakness, defect, or tendency toward sin or harmful habits.

Don't settle for failure. Lay hold on the promise!

# Life Applications

- Set daily time aside for reflection.
- List struggles or habits which rob you of peace and joy.
- Review the truths that teach good habits.
- Memorize Proverbs 16:20
- Memorize Proverbs 4:23

# The Promise of a Sound Mind

**2 Timothy 1:7** For God has not given us a spirit of fear, but of power and of love and of a sound mind.

A sound mind. Is there anything more important to us as individuals? Some would say health, but without emotional health, life loses its passion. Many things affect our mental and emotional health. There are legitimate medical causes which can affect our emotional well-being, but this book will focus on the causes and effects we can control. Plus, many physical causes begin with our attitudes and state of mind.

It's a medical fact that stress can cause physical problems. It has been directly linked to ulcers, high blood pressure, strokes, heart attacks, breakdowns in our immune systems, and many other symptoms. If we treat the symptoms, but never address the root cause, we are fighting a losing battle.

Stress is like juggling. Almost anyone can keep one ball in motion. Most people can keep two balls in the air. A few people can coordinate three. As each new ball is added, it requires more skill and concentration from the juggler. Some performances are mind-blowing. There are jugglers who can keep twelve balls up, but those types of coordinated people are rare. However, even the most skilled juggler has limitations. Toss in one ball too many and what happens? Do something which overloads the juggler's concentration and what happens? What would happen if the juggler wasn't allowed to stop? Eventually the balls are coming down. It's not if; it's when. It will either be a graceful ending, or a collapse – and all the balls will be bouncing in every direction.

What if something unexpected comes in and rams the juggler? There isn't enough skill to keep juggling when someone is unexpectedly knocked off their feet.

This is your life. You may be skilled at multitasking. You may be someone who can handle a lot of stress. Or you may be the one ball juggler that doesn't have the mind-set to handle stress at all. Whether someone's endurance to stress is great or small, everyone drops the ball when mentally overloaded.

A nervous breakdown occurs when our mind reaches the breaking point. And yes, we all have a breaking point. Once our mind reaches its endurance level, we are one event away from a collapse. The sad reality is when we reach the breaking point, we don't just drop one or two balls, we usually drop them all. During a breakdown, people have little ability to deal with life – even everyday life.

Recovery depends on how much we are able to rest our minds. For some it can be a slow and painful recovery. Think of your brain as a muscle. If a muscle is overexerted, it becomes sore and limited in its strength. A day or two of rest and it's strong and healthy again. A sore muscle only needs a few days of rest, but a pulled muscle may need weeks to recover. A torn muscle may need months to recover. Some injuries never fully recover.

This can be observed in the world of emotions as well. What you train your mind to do, it will be strengthened to do. A negative person becomes adept at negative emotions, and this comes out in their personality. The same is true for a positive person. In both cases, the individual is training the mind to be stronger in the areas where it is exercised. Yes, you exercise your mind every day. Every thought is an exercise.

Patterns become behaviors and behaviors become part of our personality and character.

Some patterns of behavior put the mind under constant stress. When we feel stressed, we often look for something to blame. We want to blame other people, work, problems, or our bodies. While these may be contributing factors to our stress, we also must realize if we are stressing our minds with negative attitudes, each problem pushes us closer to the breaking point.

A positive attitude can endure much more stress because the bad attitude is already stressed. Since negative emotions must be juggled constantly, there are few mental resources left to handle real problems when they arrive. And this is a certainty. Problems will arrive.

This is why some people have little capacity to deal with problems which others overcome easily. It's also why some of us think we have more problems than others. The negative attitude does indeed have more problems, but most are self-created. Negative attitudes amplify little annoyances into perceived problems.

Though our minds may become efficient at negative emotions, this does not make us stronger emotionally. It makes our minds more likely to respond with a negative reaction. The strengthening is in the pathways of the mind. A positive person is stronger at processing every situation in a positive way. A negative attitude trains the mind to process situations in negative ways. Then the mind is looking for escape rather than resolution.

Negativity takes more energy because it creates more stress. It also creates more problems which then demand more attention. Not only do we have to deal with the new problem, but anger is introduced into the situation. Also add in a heaping measure of frustration to top off the crisis. Many times our attitude creates a conflict with other people.

As we can see, a negative attitude invites problems in from many directions. One little problem can then appear to be a mountain of issues. Sometimes this attitude creates a problem where none exists. The simple fact that life doesn't always work the way we want it to begins to appear to us as a string of problems.

Since the world doesn't revolve around our perceived needs and desires, every person must learn to respond to their ever changing environment instead of trying to reshape the world around them.

The person holding to a negative attitude spends most of their energy dealing with unnecessary spin-off problems, and then has little if any energy left to address the real issue at hand. It's no wonder the negative person becomes overwhelmed. And most of their efforts are nonproductive. By the time they finish fighting all the internal and external conflicts, they are emotionally spent and life seems out of control. The original issue has been lost in the cloud of their emotions.

At times we all are this person. Some more than others, but we all must learn to get ourselves out of this selfish state of mind and into a healthy mindset. We must also learn to recognize when we are the author of our stress and learn to adapt rather than beat the air with the fists of our complaints.

The good news is we can retrain our way of thinking. In fact, the Bible spends a great deal of time teaching us how to do this very thing. We all have weaknesses and a bent toward negative behavior. However, we have the power to overcome these things, and the scriptures teach us how. This is something which applies to everyone.

In truth, there are medical reasons why our brains get out of balance; however, even people with physical causes can benefit from healthy emotions and healthy ways of thinking.

Many cripples have trained and competed in marathons. Some have been miraculously effective and have overcome disabilities to the point where it no longer affects them. This is the attitude I want you to have while reading this book. My hope is you'll miraculously recover from damaged emotions, but even if you need medical assistance, the principles the Bible gives us can benefit you as well. There is no situation where God's promises can't benefit – except for the one who resists God's call to change.

You may even find the physical cause of your condition goes away when your attitude changes and the constant drain of energy has been removed.

Think for a moment upon the scripture that opened this chapter. God has given us a sound mind. Something greater than you backs up this promise – it is God who gives you power, love, and a sound mind. In Peter's epistle to the church he stated, "We have been given all things that pertain to life and godliness through Christ Jesus our Lord."

Don't look at the troubles of life as hindrances to victory. The Bible says our flesh and the Spirit God has given us are at war with each other and will always be so until we are fully redeemed and stand before Him. Until then, we live in a fallen world. We live in bodies corrupted by the sins of the flesh. This includes our emotions and human ways of thinking.

The Apostle Paul, the man whom God used to write two-thirds of the New Testament, lamented over his struggles. He made the statement, "Sin in my body wars against my mind, trying to bring my mind into captivity."

This is our emotional struggle. The flesh (our fallen way of thinking) wars against our minds; however, we have been given the tools to overcome. All things that pertain to life and godliness are within our reach, but we have to make a willful choice to apply these principles so we will have the power to resist the flesh. The flesh is that corrupted nature which causes each of us to crave sin, resist God, and act out in destructive ways.

I'll warn you up front, living in the sound mind is not easy. I don't know why, but it's true. We would rather be miserable than happy. Intellectually we know better, but when it comes to applying ourselves, the truth of this statement surfaces far too often. You don't think this applies to you? Have you ever hosted a pity-party? We all have. We didn't get our way on something or we feel we have been wronged and we throw a party for one. There's no music, no dancing, no laughter, and no presents. It's just ourselves, sitting with a sour look on our face, waiting for someone to notice and give us sympathy.

Does it work? Very rarely. Instead of people rallying around us, it repels others. No one wants to go to the pity-party. People don't enjoy being around the pouter. If anything, it annoys others. When we sulk, we don't benefit in any way, we are just ruining life for ourselves and others. Self-pity doesn't work. It doesn't have any benefits. But it does have consequences. Yet we continue to try to affect our world by creating a wall of sadness around us. Joy is within reach, but we have chosen to be miserable.

The sad reality is our sulking behavior strips life out of everything. How does this make sense? I'm mad because something didn't go right; therefore, I'm going to make sure nothing goes right. Our human nature is willing to sacrifice the hundreds of good things in our life because of one thing we feel is wrong.

Illogical? Yes, but it's the reality of a life rooted in the flesh. It's easy to be sad. It takes no effort to let our minds brood. To sulk, all we must do is allow ourselves to sink into self-pity. This is why we'd rather be miserable than joyful.

Everyone has problems, frustrations, and discouragements. Everyone has enemies, or at least people with whom we have conflict. It takes no effort to allow ourselves to be pulled into negative emotions through the things we don't like.

There's a saying, "Any dead fish can float downstream." To be carried by our emotions, all we must do is let ourselves go and drift where emotions carry us. If you let your mind wander, chances are it will land on a hurt or something negative and begin brooding.

It takes life to swim against the current. Look at the contrast between bitterness and love. These are two opposing forces. One is rooted in the flesh, and one has been given to us by God. Have you ever met a bitter person?

Someone who always talks about how they have been wronged, or the things that are wrong in the world? If you spend much time around a negative person, you will adopt negative attitudes. Does a negative person have life? No. Bitterness is a life-sucking emotion.

When anger is allowed to rule, it gives birth to bitterness and hatred. These emotions serve no other purpose than to search and destroy. While these may be born from a specific offense, they cannot maintain a single target, and begin attacking our own hearts and minds, and then begin targeting those around us.

Negative emotions attempt to rise up, war against our minds, and bring us under its bondage. They are weeds in the garden of our mind. Positive emotions are like fruitful plants, but they cannot thrive when they are being choked out by these weeds.

I'm a gardener. I love growing fresh vegetables on raised beds. Few things are better than taking something from the plant and have it on your plate minutes later. There is an interesting parallel between gardening and emotions. The fruitful plants have to be cultivated. Weeds do not. If a garden is left to itself, weeds choke the vegetable plants so they become unfruitful or even die off completely. At a minimum, weeds compete for the nutrients and water the plant needs. Instead of thriving, beneficial plants are fighting for survival.

Some weeds are very invasive. My greatest garden enemy is the Red Sorrel. This monster spreads secretively. One day the garden is weed-free, and the next day these destructive plants are popping up everywhere. The Red Sorrel doesn't originate in the bed. If it's growing near the bed, it sends a root through any crack or crevice. The root spreads underground and sends new roots out in every direction.

It's there, even when the leaves are absent. When the time is right, the roots begin sending up shoots and in one day my perfectly weeded garden is covered with weeds. I pick out the weeds, but as long as the root survives, the weed will come back. It's a constant battle. To stop this weed, I have to dig out the roots and find the source. Not only do I have to be concerned with my own garden bed, but I have to remove the weed outside of my garden or it will keep coming back. This is exactly what we are dealing with in our emotional life. Look at **Hebrews 12:15**

Looking carefully lest anyone fall short of the grace of God; lest any root of bitterness springing up cause trouble, and by this many become defiled.

One bitter person can defile many. Bitterness spreads. Like the weed in the garden, the root grows under the surface and when it springs up, it attempts to threaten everything around it. Even so, what springs up is the symptom and not the whole problem.

You don't have to cultivate bitterness. Just allow it to grow and it will take over. It will take over your life and then spread to the relationships around you. We all have two choices in our emotional health. Either we rule over our emotions, or our emotions will rule over us. To be ruled, do nothing and allow them to take their natural course.

This was the case in the first murder in the Bible - when Cain killed Able. Before committing the murder, God gave wise instruction to Cain when He said, "Sin crouches at the door and its desire is for you, but you should rule over it.[2]"

This is the same command we have been given. The sin that crouched at the door began as anger, grew into bitterness, and came out in the form of hatred. It was Cain's out-of-control emotions that drove his actions and destructive behavior. In his mind, he felt justified. Bitterness became the gatekeeper of his behavior, and its

---

[2] Genesis 4:7

desire is to rule and then destroy. Since negative emotions ruled, Cain committed murder because his feelings persuaded him that he was justified in his hatred.

The emotions which are influenced by our flesh desires to rule over us, too. It crouches at the door of our hearts and waits for the opportunity to launch its attack against our mind and bring us under its rule. But we have the power of God to overcome with the love God has poured into our hearts. Instead of frustration, we can live with a sound mind.

To rule over our minds and emotional health, we must take what God has given and tame the flesh. Emotions don't have the right to rule us, but they will if we allow them to reign unchallenged. The picture I'm hoping to convey is that negative emotions are a part of life. We can't deny the reality of their existence; however, we can control whether they dominate our minds, or whether we rule over them. One of the key passages to winning the war of our minds is **Philippians 4:4-8**

4 Rejoice in the Lord always. Again I will say, rejoice!

5 Let your gentleness be known to all men. The Lord *is* at hand.

6 Be anxious for nothing, but in everything by prayer and supplication, with thanksgiving, let your requests be made known to God;

7 and the peace of God, which surpasses all understanding, will guard your hearts and minds through Christ Jesus.

8 Finally, brethren, whatever things are true, whatever things *are* noble, whatever things *are* just, whatever things *are* pure, whatever things *are* lovely, whatever things *are* of good report, if *there is* any virtue and if *there is* anything praiseworthy -- meditate on these things.

Where is the battle won? Is behavior changed by our determination to no longer worry? Or to stop being angry or bitter? The victory is already yours, but it is not through human effort. The promise is that God will guard your heart and mind through Christ. Jesus began His ministry with this message, "Repent and believe the gospel."

To repent is to turn from my ways and toward God. I then receive God's kingdom by believing the promises – the gospel. The gospel is not only the call to receive eternal life, but it is also the message of living life in the kingdom of God. The above passage is part of the gospel. You are being asked to repent – or turn – from your own human efforts, and toward the commands and promises of God.

Chances are your own ways aren't working. Look up 'stress' in any bookstore. How many titles are dedicated to this topic? Frustration and stress are thieves of peace and joy, and the destroyers of lives and families.

Yet the simplicity of the gospel is to repent and believe. This applies to every command and promise of God. God commands to rejoice always. How do you define always? Is it possible to rejoice and complain? Problems are real, but rejoicing puts them into the proper perspective. If I believe God is directing my steps, I must learn to rejoice in the good and the bad. I say 'bad' from the perspective of human reasoning, but the truth is that nothing is bad if we are walking in God's plan.

I've never met a defeated Christian who purposed to rejoice always. Yes, we all have problems, but what makes one person a defeatist and another person optimistic? It all centers around attitude. This is the purpose of rejoicing. It forces our attitude in the right direction by acknowledging the Lord's hand of providence.

This is something we'll explore as we move through this book, but even if we don't understand God's reasoning, we can still rejoice. Rejoicing is looking at God's eternal purposes and praising the Lord as He moves us toward the goal of inheriting His kingdom.

The next principle in Philippians above tells us to be anxious for nothing. Can you stop the anxiety simply by being told not to be anxious? Most of us cannot. This is why the command to not be anxious is given along with the application of God's principles to our lives. We lose anxiety by approaching God in prayer through thanksgiving. It begins with an attitude that rejoices – even when we don't understand why and can't see the end result. In fact, you will seldom know the end result until you reach the end.

Most Christians never see God's completed work in their lives because they cannot trust Him when the going is tough.

We naturally want to escape problems and hardships, and often turn back before the victory has been revealed. It may be a short trial or a long hardship. If we believe God and trust Him, we'll always stand amazed at His power to bring good out of every circumstance. If we don't believe, we don't see the reward, and never find the good. Life is hard, but harder when we miss the goodness of God. The promise is only assured to those who trust Him enough to remain faithful until the Lord reveals His purposes.

Through prayer and supplication with thanksgiving, we make our requests known to God. We'll delve into thanksgiving in a later chapter, but understand that thankfulness is the foundation all prayers must be built upon. Let me repeat this for emphasis. Thanksgiving is the foundation all prayers must be built upon. Otherwise we are seeking our will and asking God to conform to our ways. A thankful heart trusts the Lord while walking through the valley of difficulty. Praying, "God, get me out of this," is not a prayer of faith.

A person who becomes internally focused will never have peace. 'Woe is me' is internally focused. 'God give me,' is an internally focused prayer. 'Why is this happening,' is internally focused. The more I focus on my problems, the bigger they become. The more I focus on myself, the more desperate I become to satisfy my selfish will.

Have you ever met someone with deep-rooted emotional problems? I have, and each time 'me' is at the center of their world. 'I' didn't get treated right. 'I' was offended. 'I' didn't get the respect I deserved. 'I' have this problem, that problem, etc. When we withdraw into ourselves, it becomes a dark pit with little hope. But when we begin to look outward, we then have the opportunity to put our life into a healthier perspective.

For example, when people go to third-world countries and see the desperate conditions and poverty in which people live, they no longer feel deprived because they don't have some of the luxuries that once seemed important. When we see the pain and needs of others, our petty problems lose significance.

This is but a glimpse of what it means to look outside of ourselves. As each of us begin to learn what it means to look to Christ, the Author and Finisher of our faith, life truly begins to gain perspective. In light of eternity, does it really matter if I didn't get that promotion? When I see the promised inheritance to the faithful, does it really matter if someone didn't follow through with a promise on earth? Does this world have significance when it comes to my gratification? As the Apostle Peter said, "Seeing all these things will one day be dissolved, what manner of persons ought you to be in holy conduct and godliness?"

It's a daily effort to live for eternity and not for this life only. If something doesn't have eternal significance, it is petty, and should be viewed as such. You and I must begin each day by recognizing our natural tendency to become internally focused, and we must do something to change this. Each time self becomes the focus, it's a reminder to turn from 'me' and adopt an outward perspective.

If nothing in this life matters in light of eternity, how ought we to live? What should we live for? What things deserve significance? We have the answer – pray with thanksgiving as we make requests known to God and look to Jesus as the finish line so we are not discouraged in our souls.[3]

When faced with His most difficult trial, Jesus said, "What shall I say – Father save Me? It is for this purpose I came into the world."

This is the eternal perspective. You too have a purpose. Each of us are being led toward God's plan, yet we tend to be so focused on our comfort that we miss the purposes of God. While we are crying, "Save me from this trial," God is trying to show us the real goal – eternal significance. It's far too easy to be distracted by meaningless cares and then to miss the real purpose of our lives. Jesus warned that many will allow their lives to be choked by the cares of this life and other things coming in to distract them from eternal value. These are the people whose lives become unfruitful.

We must take steps to not allow meaningless cares to become overvalued, and recognize God has eternal value in mind. When our perspective includes the eternal, this gives us the heart to pray with thanksgiving. And as we do, we stand upon the promise that He will become the guard of our hearts and minds.

This is the life of faith. Do you believe God? Do I believe God? If we do, then claim the promise of peace which has been given to each believer. There are times when we'll have to look beyond our circumstances and say, "I believe your word, Lord. I will rejoice and be thankful, and I receive your promise of peace which goes beyond my understanding. I submit to your will and receive your promise to guard my heart and mind."

---

[3] Hebrews 12:2-3

It is God's work. Your job is not to guard your heart and mind from anxiety, fear, and trouble. It is God's job to do this. Your job is to turn from your way and believe God. It is your job to reject the call of anxiety, fear, anger, and other negative emotions. As you surrender in obedience, you will experience God's peace and protection. But we can't have God's peace while living for our own ways.

The final thought given in the passage above teaches us how to train our minds. Meditate on these things: whatever is true, noble, just, pure, lovely, of a good report, and anything of virtue and praiseworthy.

Don't expect peace through gossip. The mind won't be guarded if we meditate on our anger, lust, lies, bad reports, or any other negative thing that plagues our minds.

Sadly, each of us has the tendency to dwell on the sinful and negative, but then we want to experience peace. The first step of peace is to submit our minds to the pure things of godliness and turn away (repent) from the things which are contrary to God.

The promise of God is a sound mind. Believe this, claim it through obedience, and let's explore the ways to root the thieves of peace out of our lives.

# Life Applications

- When self-pity begins, stop and evaluate what's important in life:
    - Ask yourself if what bothers you has life-long or eternal significance?
    - Ask yourself if this disappointment is important enough to cast off the rest of life's good things?
    - Is robbing myself of joy a benefit or will it lead to any benefit?
- **Self-evaluate:** what attitudes or behaviors are choking out positive things in my life?
- Am I cultivating bitterness?
- Memorize Philippians 4:8.
- Spend a few minutes each week to identifying things that fulfill Philippians 4:8.
- Spend time each morning thinking upon at least one thing that fulfills this passage. Don't allow your mind to wander away from positive meditation.
- Meditate (or think upon) something that fulfills this passage while you are waiting to fall asleep each night.
- Make this a daily morning and evening practice and a life-long habit. Even if you don't feel like it, discipline yourself to think upon these things.

# Preparing for War

The Bible states, the flesh wars against our minds and attempts to bring us back into bondage. This means our flesh rises up and attempts to dominate our ways of thinking based on a physical standard. Life is more than getting what we want, experiencing temporary pleasures, and acquiring things. It is more than getting our way and retaliating for wrongs.

If the flesh could satisfy, the rich would be content, the beautiful would be confident, and the selfish would be happy. But history has proven true the words of scripture, "The eyes of man are never satisfied."[4] However, those who live by faith truly experience the words of the imprisoned Apostle Paul, "I've learned to be content, whatever the circumstance."[5]

Even when we experience godly peace and true contentment, our flesh still waits for the opportunity to take advantage of a moment of weakness in order to reintroduce its futile way of thinking. The flesh is in bondage to a temporal world.

Life in the flesh is a brief moment. It should be no surprise that the flesh, which is temporal, is bound by a way of thinking which is only based upon the here and now. So even if you understand the reality of eternity, you'll still be tempted to fall back into the old ways of thinking.

Don't be surprised if you struggle. We all struggle. Today's victory will not be tomorrow's victory. Each day is a new battle. Though the war never ends, the promise that we are more than conquerors becomes a reality.

The Bible often uses the illustration of war when it comes to the Christian life. The war is not against people or outward things, but it's fought within our own flesh.

---

[4] Proverbs 27:20
[5] Philippians 4:11

There are two sources we battle against. One is described in **2 Corinthians 10:4-5**

> [4] For the weapons of our warfare *are* not carnal but mighty in God for pulling down strongholds,
>
> [5] casting down arguments and every high thing that exalts itself against the knowledge of God, bringing every thought into captivity to the obedience of Christ,

This passage affirms what we've already discussed. We overcome through the Spirit and not through human effort. As Jesus said, "The flesh profits you nothing." Victory is not found by trying harder, or implementing a plan of action through carnal (or fleshly) actions. This is why people may improve behaviors for a while, but keep slipping back into old habits or addictions. Our flesh is weak and incapable of living by a spiritual standard.

All temptation is made through the flesh, but victory comes through walking in the Spirit. This is why Galatians 5:16 tells us, "Walk in the Spirit and you will not fulfill the lusts of the flesh."

One source of our battle is spiritual in nature. **Ephesians 6:12** tells us:

> [12] For we do not wrestle against flesh and blood, but against principalities, against powers, against the rulers of the darkness of this age, against spiritual *hosts* of wickedness in the heavenly *places.*

People may appear to be the source of our problems, but often they are tools of spiritual wickedness. We also can become tools of spiritual wickedness. Anyone who allows the flesh to control their life is not walking in the Spirit and is subject to manipulation by spiritual wickedness.

No one is above temptation and no one is immune to doing evil. When someone stops living by God's spiritual power, the only other source is the flesh – and the flesh is corrupted by sin. As the Bible states, sin dwells in the members of our flesh and can be used to capture our minds for ungodly purposes. This is why Christians fall. Sometimes they do things that are very unchristian-like. This is also why the Bible warns believers in the church to stop warring among one another lest they devour one another. Christians aren't immune to the flesh, and a flesh driven believer can act out in harmful ways.

To deter Christians from becoming flesh driven, both Jesus and the apostles warned believers that we will be held accountable for what is done in our bodies. We are to subjugate the flesh to Christ and not allow ourselves to be controlled by the flesh. This is why the above passage warns us about spiritual wickedness, and why 2 Corinthians warns us the real battle is not fought through the flesh.

The flesh can be used against us by spiritual powers, but we overcome by the might given to us by God. That might is available when we walk in the Spirit. Satan attempts to draw us into the flesh, but we resist by submitting ourselves to God[6], for if we walk in the Spirit, we will not fulfill the lusts of the flesh.[7]

Spiritual wickedness wars against our soul by trying to draw our focus off the Spirit and into the lusts of the flesh.[8] Lust does not only mean sensuality. The lust of the flesh can be greed, bitterness, hatred, immorality, and any other temptation that draws us out of our walk in the Spirit.

We battle spiritual wickedness with the spiritual weapons God has given us. This is also how we battle the flesh. Whether it's an outside attack against us, or a temptation from within, the attack comes through the flesh, but victory is found through the Spirit.

Let me reiterate this important truth. Our victory only comes through the Spirit. For the most part, the attack on our souls comes from our own sinful desires. Even without a spiritual attack, our flesh still craves sin and must be

---

[6] James 4:7-8
[7] Galatians 5:16
[8] 1 Peter 2:11

brought under subjection to Christ. Look at **Romans 7:19-25**

> 19 For the good that I will *to do,* I do not do; but the evil I will not *to do,* that I practice.
>
> 20 Now if I do what I will not *to do,* it is no longer I who do it, but sin that dwells in me.
>
> 21 I find then a law, that evil is present with me, the one who wills to do good.
>
> 22 For I delight in the law of God according to the inward man.
>
> 23 But I see another law in my members, warring against the law of my mind, and bringing me into captivity to the law of sin which is in my members.
>
> 24 O wretched man that I am! Who will deliver me from this body of death?
>
> 25 I thank God -- through Jesus Christ our Lord! So then, with the mind I myself serve the law of God, but with the flesh the law of sin.

This was written by the apostle we would consider an icon of Christianity – Paul. God used the Apostle Paul to pen two-thirds of the New Testament, yet he struggled just as you and I do. He lamented that even though he knew to do good, and desired to do good, another force was working in his body of flesh. Though he was redeemed and had a new spiritual nature, his flesh remained corrupted by sin.

The sin abiding in his own flesh rose up and warred against his mind, causing him to slip back into a fleshly way of thinking and acting. He lamented his failure and weakened condition and said, "Who will rescue me from this body of death?"

Paul then gave the answer to his question – the flesh can only serve sin, but I thank God that through Jesus Christ, my mind has the power to serve the law of God. In other words, the flesh cannot be made spiritual. Instead, the flesh is overcome through the power of Christ – a power we have been given and we can experience daily when walking in the Spirit.

When the flesh rules, the war spreads to those around the person who is flesh-driven, but the real battle is won in the heart of the believer who submits to God and walks in the Spirit.

Without submission to God, there can be no victory.

Let's look at the word-picture of war. Think about World War II and the battle to defeat Hitler. This dictator's goal was to rule the world. He believed he was a man of destiny and the Third Reich would dominate the earth for a thousand years.

When Hitler began his campaign, what did the world do? Nothing. And he gained strength. With ease he took over the weaker countries around him. Once he grew to a strength which threatened the world, no one could ignore the reality of war. When the US entered the war, there was much uncertainty as to whether Hitler could be stopped. It was a hard and long war. But what happened when Hitler lost his first battle? He was no longer invincible and began to lose his stronghold.

Each country he lost was a difficult battle, but one by one, the countries he took over were liberated. With each liberation, the enemy lost strength.

This is the picture of the spiritual warfare in our own lives. The battle is fought in our minds and hearts. When someone feels oppressed by their emotions, the enemy seems invincible. By human effort, this is true, but God has promised to reveal His power in us. Through His word we are given the spiritual power and strategies to defeat an enemy that is greater than we are.

With each victory, the enemy grows weaker, and though the war may be a lifelong struggle, the daily battle won't be insurmountable once the word of God becomes our fortress, and the stronghold of the enemy has been broken.

The enemy is your own human nature. People often think Satan is the enemy, and though he is a threat, his power is through the flesh. The devil can't oppress us without our allowing him to do so. Most deception is intended to persuade us into giving him a stronghold without realizing we are doing so. He is the master manipulator. He manipulates us with temptation, but it is our own actions which turns temptation from thoughts to reality.

This is a Christian book. The focus is on applying God's word so we can experience the promise of becoming more than a conqueror. You will experience victory if you live by the principles we'll discuss from the Bible. However, don't fall into the trap of believing your problems are the work of the devil.

The Bible puts little emphasis on the devil. Consider the words of Paul, "When I do what I know is wrong...it is sin which dwells in my members (body of flesh)." It wasn't Satan oppressing him; it was the sin already present within his own body of flesh[9]. We are warned not to be ignorant of Satan's devices. This is so we are not deceived into giving him a place. He has no power to overcome the believer, for greater is He who is in you (Christ) than he that is in the world (Satan).[10]

Paul was an Apostle of Christ – what we would consider the height of spiritual maturity. Yet he struggled just as we do. To blame an outside force blinds us to the real problem – we must deal with our own behavior and take the steps necessary to live in self-control. Emotions are the hardest part of self-control. The solution is not to blame demons, but to know the life-changing truth of scripture, and to apply it to daily living.

We do this by taking back the strongholds sin has brought under its rule. By sin, I'm referring to the actions of our flesh which opposes the truth of God. If God says, "Do not let your heart be troubled," but we have embraced the

---

[9] Romans 7:21
[10] 1 John 4:4

trouble of our hearts, we have submitted ourselves to the sin dwelling in our flesh and are now allowing it to rule over our hearts. Anxiety and other strongholds of the flesh then become the driving force of our lives.

Does this mean we have sinned when we worry or something troubling has occurred? Do we have to deny reality in order to be within God's perfect design? Certainly not!

Some things have to be addressed and worry is a natural human emotion. Problems have to be faced, but we must learn to do so in a healthy way. Dealing with troubling situations does not mean we are ruled by worry, and the command to be anxious for nothing does not mean we deny the existence of problems.

The remainder of this book will examine how the Bible addresses these things and how we live within the promise, "God has given us power, love, and a sound mind." Joy, peace, love, and soundness of mind are promises God gives when we follow biblical principles.

Always keep this expectation in mind: God's principles are easy to understand, but hard to live by. Do not allow this to become an excuse for failure, but rather the realization that diligence is required.

It goes against human thinking to overcome, but this is where the rewards of life are found. Our natural tendency is to allow our feelings to sweep us down stream. Fortunately, they have the power to carry us, but not the power to force us. We have the power to drive against the current. But to do this, we must know what God has taught us in the scriptures, and must be willing to both surrender to the Lord's word and be willing to stand against the flesh.

With this being said, let's discover the victorious principles of the word that empower us to be more than conquerors.

# Life Applications

- Think about something you struggle with - worry, lust, anger, bitterness, etc. Submit these things to God and pray for a heart which trusts the Lord with your temptation.
- Memorize James 4:6-10.
- When you feel the desire to give into your flesh, recite the above passage from James. Draw near to God as you submit your weakness to Him and then resist your flesh by trusting in the Lord.
- Think about people who have wronged you and consider the fact that they are in bondage to the flesh. Forgive and pray for their deliverance as you consider that you also are seeking deliverance from the flesh's control in your life.
- Go back and review the Life Applications from previous chapters. Practice them so they don't slip from your focus.

# The Blessed Attitude

Many things in life are outside of our control. Life throws us many curves. Hardships befall us. People in our lives may be difficult. There are so many opportunities for failure, but only few opportunities for success. The real question is, do our circumstances determine our success or failure.

The answer is a resounding, No!

How is it that two children can be raised in the same difficult living conditions and environment, yet one will rise above it, and the other will become a victim who carries their negative experiences into the next generation? The opposite is also true. How is it that two kids can be raised in a nurturing environment, but one will become bitter and the other will thrive in life?

The truth is that no one has a perfect nurturing environment. People who have a good life can always find negative things to focus on, and people raised in a cruel world can find good and climb out of the cycle of failure. What is the key that opens the door to a good course for our lives?

Attitude.

Things will enter each of our lives we cannot control, but one thing we can control is our own attitude. And our attitude is the blueprint for how we build our lives in the world in which we live. This is by God's design.

The Lord has promised two things we can anchor our hopes upon.

One is that God promises He will not allow us to endure more than we can bear. This promise is regarding temptation from without. God does not promise He will not allow us to self-destruct. If we are determined to find the bad in life and are determined to milk negativism for all it's worth, God will not stop us. God doesn't protect us from our own rebellion, but He does protect us from the evils around us. When I say protect, it is our hearts that are protected.

What's more, the Bible says to be strong in the Lord and the power of His might. This means we have unlimited strength if we put our focus on seeking God and allowing Him to guide us to the good in every circumstance.

God will not allow hardships to overcome our faith, but He will allow hardships to break us from trusting in the flesh. If you are relying on the power of your might, God's promise doesn't apply. The Lord doesn't promise to protect our fleshly way of living. Sometimes we have more than we can bear because we are trusting in our strength instead of God's unlimited power given through the Spirit.

Evil cannot destroy our heart, but evil within our heart can destroy us. And negativism is evil nurtured within our heart. We are the cultivators of what thrives in our heart.

Brooding produces nothing good. The heart is like a garden. We can plant poison ivy, thorns, and harmful plants in our garden, but why would we want to? Yet this is what many of us do in our own hearts. Something harmful will spring up, and instead of weeding it out, we rush to water it, cultivate it, grow it into something powerful, and then wonder why it is affecting our lives.

If we are grumbling under our breath, complaining about everything, murmuring, and cultivating a negative attitude, we'll reap these things in our lives. The Bible warns that what we sow, we will also reap. If I'm constantly walking around and grumbling under my breath, what can I expect to reap through my emotions? I'll reap what I am sowing and nurturing – a negative grumbling spirit.

I have never seen a happy grumbler. I have never seen a broody person with a joyful attitude. The more I brood, the darker my attitude becomes. Have you ever listened to the testimonies of people who 'just snapped'? Those who commit atrocities have a history of brooding. They allow what harms them to dominate their thoughts and it grows into an obsession. The more they brood, the more stressed they feel. They become time-bombs that are only one incident away from exploding.

On a smaller scale, every person can become a bomb maker. If our attitude puts us on edge, it doesn't take much to set us off. Brooding builds up the pressure and then we start expecting negative things from people, and we react as though everything is an offense. Sometimes innocent comments are misinterpreted as an attack. This causes our negative attitude to react based on our internal turmoil, rather than upon the intention of the person we are reacting against.

The negative spirit imposes their feelings onto others. This causes them to interpret innocent mistakes or comments as an attack. It also causes the negative person to view petty disagreements as momentous. Instead of shrugging off little annoyances, the negative spirit goes to war.

While few people make the news, many people are time-bombs. They are one incident away from having a temper explosion, emotional meltdown, deep depression, or any other outlet for their emotional reaction. Notice I said 'reaction', not 'response'. There is a difference. Most people react to their environment. Circumstances create an automatic reaction which drives their lives. Yet the sound mind knows how to respond to circumstances.

Negative attitudes can only react. Only positive attitudes have the power to respond.

We have the power to stop, consider an appropriate response, and resolve the problem. But this is only possible when we are in control of ourselves instead of being controlled by our circumstances. Or being controlled by our negative attitudes.

It's important to reiterate this again. We project our attitude on others without even realizing it. A good attitude assumes the other person is thinking positively, but the bad attitude interprets negativism from a person even when it is not present. A dishonest person doesn't trust others, in the same way, a negative person believes those around them are also negative.

While doing some interim preaching in a church, I noticed a storm brewing among some members. There was a lot of backbiting going on and I decided to address the situation by explaining the Bible's command to love the brethren. I looked at what it means to love, and what love does not allow us to do to our brethren. After the message I received two reactions. Those who knew nothing about the turmoil going on said they felt inspired and encouraged to express Christian love.

Those who were manufacturing division became angry. I received angry phone calls and was accused of spewing venom from the pulpit. One person quoted me as saying something I never even thought. He was so insistent that I listened to a recording of the message. The offensive things some people heard were never spoken.

How can two groups of people hear such different messages? One expected to be blessed from the scriptures, but the other expected offense. Their attitudes affected how they interpreted what they heard. In fact, those with negative attitudes heard things which were never said.

How many offenses in life are similar in nature? It isn't what is said, it is what is assumed that offends people. "He just thinks... I know she's mad at me because she didn't speak...He's doing that to get under my skin...I can tell she doesn't like me by the look in her eye."

All of these are assumptions. Most are wrong. Yet we can manufacture conflict so the assumption becomes reality. We project our attitudes on others and this can build up or tear down relationships.

The second promise of God is that all things work for our good. God did not promise all things in our life would be good (that is from the human perspective) but that it would produce good. This is something I'll refer to again as we move through this book. God is looking for your good – not merely here on earth, but good from the eternal perspective.

We get so shortsighted that we think a setback or loss of something temporal is a tragedy.

Many years ago, a local newspaper covered a story on a man's reaction to an accident. Someone rear-ended his boat in traffic. He snapped and attacked the man and severely beat him. His action sent him to prison. Because of a scuff on his fishing boat, he was willing to attempt to kill the person who accidentally caused the damage.

The real irony is that by now his boat is probably in a junkyard somewhere – along with thousands of other boats which have aged to the point of uselessness. Is a possession bound for the junkyard worthy of our life?

Life is filled with disappointments. I may lose my job, lose a ball game, miss that promotion, or any other thing I think is important in this 70-80 year life. Are these truly worth an emotional investment? If I'm cheated, will it matter in the course of my life? How will it look in light of eternity? Is it worth the hatred, bitterness, or desire for revenge? Is it worthy of my sorrow and despair? Is self-destructive behavior the answer to a problem? Any problem?

No. Nothing in this life is worthy of the value we place on it. As the Apostle Paul once said, "The sufferings of this life are not even worthy to be compared to the glory which shall be revealed in us." By 'us' he is referring to those who have given up temporal things in order to live for eternity.

No suffering is even worthy of our comparison. Therefore, we should not be investing our lives into our sufferings, irritations, annoyances, frustrations, disappointments, or any other thing that displeases us in this life. Our focus should not be on what we have lost, but what we are gaining. The focus has to be on where we are going – and that requires having a direction to go.

See the goal and begin walking that way. What is your goal in cultivating a healthy emotional and spiritual life? We must cultivate an eternal perspective. This will affect our attitudes and values in every area of life.

# Cultivating a Positive Outlook

It's important to have an accurate understanding of the power of attitudes. The attitude itself doesn't create a mystical power which makes things happen, for the power is not in you. Good attitudes change our heart to look for good and receive good, while negative attitudes have the opposite effect.

Many New Age circles and various religions operate on the belief that we create reality by our thoughts. They falsely believe positive thoughts *create* good things and negative thoughts *create* bad things. While it is true positive attitudes find more opportunities and have better success than negative attitudes, I'd like to examine this from a more accurate perspective – a perspective which directly affects each of our lives.

Simply by observing people, it is clear those with positive attitudes find good more often than those with bad attitudes. Is this the power of the mind to alter the universe? Or is there a deeper meaning?

I've often wondered about this belief. Can you imagine, six-billion people altering reality to suit their own desires? If this were possible, the world would be a mass of chaos and confusion.

The truth is, we have been born into our specific circumstance, and we have to build ourselves upon our faith as we respond to our unique situation. Though I believe the Bible's claim that God foreordained my life before the foundation of the world, I also believe the scriptures which say, "Choose this day a blessing or a curse." It is God's desire to bless, and indeed He has built His blessings into every life. This is also true for the people who seem to have been dealt a bad hand in life.

It's not the bad hand we've been dealt that ruins our lives. Life appears sour when we lack the willingness to look for the blessings all around us. Let's look through the lens of both the negative attitude and the positive one and see how our attitude affects the outcome of life.

### The Negative Lens.

A negative person is focused on what? They gaze upon the things in life that annoy them. A negative heart focuses on what is wrong in the world around them, how they have been wronged, offended, lack the types of opportunities they wanted, aren't pretty enough, skinny enough, rich enough, educated enough, and the list goes on and on.

When something goes wrong they cross their arms, plop down, and say 'woe is me'. A negative attitude focuses on what bothers them, and this becomes all they see. A grumbling heart is stuck on what offends and it blinds the grumbler to the good around them. Their attitude strangles relationships and blinds them to anything but the offense. This negative mind-set becomes a cycle – for it creates more offenses while also clinging to the past ones.

All the grumbler sees are the things which are wrong. Indeed there are things wrong. Every one of us has many situations in our lives we do not like and wish we could change. But when the things which offend become our focus, life revolves around a cycle of negativism.

So is it the negative thoughts which create negative circumstances? No. Everyone has negative circumstances, and some people endure horrible things, yet overcome. The truth is, negative circumstances are part of living in a fallen world, and it will always be around you. The problem with the negative attitude is that it invites the passing trouble to take up residence.

### The Positive Lens.

The positive attitude has the opposite effect on the individual. You've probably met someone who has gone through a tragedy and yet they seem happy and joyful. I've heard others ask these types of people, "How can you handle what you've been through so well?"

The truth is, they have probably shed many tears. They sorrowed over the loss they endured, but they dealt with it in a healthy way. Instead of making the tragedy their prison, they used it as steps to climb higher. They overcame – not because it didn't hurt – but because they looked for the good on the other side.

The Bible says we should look to the attitude of Christ, "who for the joy set before Him endured the cross while despising its shame." We are commanded to consider His life so we are not ensnared by the cares of life, we don't become discouraged in our souls, and so we can also endure through joy.[11]

Consider what the Bible says about Jesus' view of the cross. Jesus despised the cross. He hated it. He knew it was the source of His pain and suffering, yet He endured – not by focusing on the cross, but by looking beyond it to the joy that lies ahead. He endured what He despised by focusing on the good that would come through His suffering. And we are told to look to His example so we don't become discouraged in our souls.

Did Jesus' positive attitude change His circumstances? No. The cross still stood between Him and the goal. There was no other way but to endure what He was about to suffer. But His attitude changed. This is one reason we are told Jesus can identify with us as our High Priest, for He suffered and was tempted in all ways like us.

If we look at Jesus' prayer before going to the cross, we see a wonderful example for our encouragement. He was alone. His closest friends did not take His foretelling of the coming suffering seriously, and when He invited them to pray with Him, they fell asleep. He woke them, but they fell asleep again. After His prayer time, He sat beside His disciples and said, "Take your rest now." He then waited alone until His persecutors came to arrest Him before waking them again.

---

[11] Hebrews 12:1

The Blessed Attitude

But I want to focus on His prayer as written in Matthew 26. Jesus prayed three times for deliverance. He began by pleading with our Heavenly Father to take the cup of suffering away. He ended by acknowledging the will of the Father as something to be obeyed over His own. In the next prayer, we see His words surrendering to that perfect will. The final prayer was an acknowledgment that He must endure this suffering, and His willingness to follow the plan that led to our redemption. Though He knew this ahead of time, He still had to struggle through His human emotions.

When Jesus said, "Not my will but yours," an angel strengthened Him.[12] Though the temptation kept pounding at His will, Jesus looked to the will of the Father as the source of good and placed His hope in the Father's plan.

This is how we also approach life. There is nothing wrong with asking God for a way of escape unless it is to request God follow our will instead of us following Him. Sometimes we must pass through the suffering for a greater good. And unlike Christ, we don't have the foreknowledge to see the reason behind our trials. But this doesn't change how we approach the pains of life.

Sometimes God delivers us, but other times God gives us strength from heaven to endure it. It is not until we look back that we can see the good God intended. Add to this, the Lord does not correct this fallen world before us simply because we become Christians and are no longer part of its ways. We still must endure what the world around us endures, but we show the hope beyond the suffering. We endure with joy, because unlike the unbeliever, we have a glimpse into eternity and know God's goodness awaits. And we also know the promise if we suffer for His will, we shall also reign with Him.[13]

A negative person can't see the strength of God offered from heaven because they are not looking at the Author and

---

[12] Luke 22:43
[13] Romans 8:17, 2 Timothy 2:12

Finisher of our faith. They are looking at the world and cannot see the comforting hand of God. Nor can they see the joy set before them, which gives them the strength to endure. This is why the Bible says, "The joy of the Lord is your strength."[14]

Even though the one with the right attitude may have to endure suffering, they have eyes to see what the negative attitude cannot. In the midst of this fallen world is the goodness of God. The blessing can be obscured by the curse of a fallen world, but the one with the right attitude is looking for the blessing – and will always find it.

The blessing may be a way of escape. It might be strength to endure. It might be the hidden door of opportunity. It may also be the rewards of eternity. The right attitude is always rewarded. The right attitude also is always looking for good and finds it. Our positive attitude does not recreate reality, nor does it create what we desire. A positive attitude gives us eyes to look for the good – even among bad. It creates in our hearts the desire to find God's blessing among the chaos and difficulties around us.

A good attitude doesn't change our circumstances. It changes our focus. When we are looking for the good we know is out there, we will eventually find it. But a person who only looks at what is bad will be overwhelmed with the smorgasbord of bad all around them. The world is corrupted by sin and until God redeems all things, creation remains fallen and filled with troubles. But God will not allow us to be overcome by evil, so He has woven His good throughout a fallen world. But it is only found by those with eyes to see it.

Even an unbeliever can have a good attitude and look for good and the window of opportunity, but it doesn't change the fact that this is God's design. Or as Jesus stated, "Your Heavenly Father makes the sun rise on the just and unjust. He makes the rain to fall on the just and unjust." In other words, good and bad are in this fallen world. Until we

---

[14] Nehemiah 8:10

awake in eternity, we have to endure this world. Yet the goodness of the Lord can be found to any who will seek it.

What the pagan religions think they are creating with positive attitudes is actually the goodness of the Lord given to all. While they don't have the promise of God's inheritance, the goodness of God is seen by all – both the just and the unjust. Some blessings are only within God's plan and provided to the Christian, but benevolent grace is given to all.

This especially applies to you. If you are cultivating a negative attitude, you will see the fallen world and the things that bother you. Suffering will be your housemate. But if you cultivate a good attitude, good will be found, even in the midst of hardship. Some think blessed people are a magnet for good, but the truth is blessed people are those who have cultivated the right heart and look for good.

A positive attitude must be cultivated. A cultivator uproots what is undesirable while nurturing what is good. A cultivated heart doesn't just happen. It must be an intentional effort.

# Life Applications

- Memorize Hebrews 12:1-3
- Memorize Romans 8:28
- Think about what is beyond your problems. Think about the promise of standing before the Lord. Think about the promise of bringing good into your life even in painful circumstances.
- When you feel frustrated or overwhelmed, stop and remember to look for good.
- When you get upset, ask yourself, "Am I reacting or responding?"
- In each situation ask, "Am I being controlled by circumstances, or am I exercising my God given right to control my responses to circumstances?"
- Remind yourself you are not trying to be strong, but are yielding yourself to God's purposes, knowing He will send strength from heaven. It is His strength which gives endurance, and it is His joy which becomes our strength.

# Freedom to Rule

We have been given the freedom to rule our emotions and bodies of flesh. One of the challenges of life is determining what is truly freedom and what is a trap of deception.

Proverbs states, "Folly appears to be joy to the one who is destitute of discernment," and that "his own iniquities entrap him and he is caught in the cords of his sin." In other words, giving ourselves over to ungodly behavior may seem like freedom, but it is a snare. While foolish actions and sinful desires masquerade as liberty, they are luring us into bondage, and then we become slaves to our behaviors. Instead of ruling, our sins can become our rulers.

What seems like freedom from the perspective of the flesh may be the friendly hand of bondage. The Bible says the kisses of an enemy are deceitful, and the one who flatters is setting a net for our feet.[15] The trap of bondage presents itself as a friend until the shackles are in place. While this is true for deceitful people, it is even more true for our own deceitful heart. Consider the words of **Jeremiah 17:9-10**

> 9 " The heart *is* deceitful above all *things,* And desperately wicked; Who can know it?
> 10 I, the LORD, search the heart, *I* test the mind, Even to give every man according to his ways, According to the fruit of his doings.

Our greatest deceiver is the human heart. The heart is where our passions, desires, and emotions reside. While the wisdom of the world says, "Follow your heart," God has declared, "The one who trusts in his own heart is a fool, but whoever walks wisely will be delivered." (Proverbs 28:26) To see the truth of this, look at the consequences around us. Prisons are filled with people who followed their heart. Adultery, theft, murder, manipulation, and any other sinful

---

[15] Proverbs 29:5, Proverbs 27:6

behavior comes from those who are following the desires of their heart.

According to Jesus, sin arises from the heart. He stated, "Out of the heart proceeds evil thoughts, murders, adulteries, sexual immorality, thefts, false witnesses, and blasphemies."[16] Yet, Jesus also said, "He who believes in Me, out of his heart will flow rivers of living water."[17] When the Bible uses the word 'he' in the general sense, it is like the word 'man'. It applies to mankind as a whole – including women. This passage applies to all people and genders.

How can we trust our heart, seeing it can produce either sin, or waters of life? We can't. It isn't the heart we are trusting, it's the Lord who reveals the true motives of the heart and gives to us according to the fruit of our doings. Those who trust in the human heart will reap the fruit of sinful flesh. Those who trust in the Lord will reap the fruit of the Spirit and see the life of God flowing through them.

While it may appear subtle at first glance, there is a vast difference between trusting in our heart and trusting in the Lord. There is a big difference between letting our hearts lead us and allowing the Lord to lead our hearts. The heart is selfish by nature; therefore, it will always look for self-gratification.

The move of the Spirit in our heart often calls us to set aside our quest for satisfaction, and beckons us to follow the leading of the Lord. We must trust in the promise that we will be satisfied through Him in the end.

The human heart searches for satisfaction through gratification, yet this is not possible. Gratification is the saturation of our desires, but it cannot fill the longing of our heart. If it could, money would satisfy the rich. Immorality would satisfy our lusts. Revenge would satisfy our sense of justice. The truth is, none of these ever satisfy. There may be a moment of perceived satisfaction, but it quickly fades,

---

[16] Matthew 15:19

[17] John 7:38

leaving us longing for something more. Oftentimes, it leaves us with guilt instead of satisfaction.

When a reporter looked at the Rockefellers and saw the incomprehensible wealth, he asked, "How much is enough?"

John D. Rockefeller answered, "Just a little bit more."

This is the condition of the human heart. Enough is never enough. If you can't learn to be satisfied with your life now, you will never be satisfied with life, regardless of any amount of wealth or gratification. When life settles into a norm, a discontented heart will always find another source of discontentment. This is why the Bible says, "The eyes of man are never satisfied."[18]

Like the kisses of an enemy, letting go of control can give the illusion of freedom. An enemy gives the pretense of friendship through flattering words and false affection. Our foes do this to gain a position of strength before launching an attack.

Your emotions befriend you with desires, and passions that give the false sense of freedom and satisfaction. Letting go seems freeing at first, but when the consequences roll in, our lack of restraint becomes the chains of bondage.

It always feels good to let lust rule our lives – at first. Releasing anger feels like a relief at the moment of release, but what happens to unrestrained anger. Not only does it harm those around us, but it quickly becomes the master over our lives.

Emotions, desires, and passions *can* make good servants, but they make terrible masters. Just as we saw earlier, these desire to rule us, but we must rule over them. Otherwise, we will be driven by our desires instead of being led by the Spirit. Emotions, desires, and passions have a place in life, but their roles should be limited. These should be subject to us, not the other way around. In the lives of most people, these things step out of their God-given roles and usurp authority over us that should not belong to them.

---

[18] Proverbs 27:20

Why does the violent man abuse his wife? Why do mothers abuse children? Or gamblers squander away the provisions of their families? Name any destructive behavior and at the center of the problem lies a heart ruled by passion. The heart is either submitted to God, or ruled by passions. We either exercise our volition to do what is right – regardless of how we feel – or we allow our heart to be ruled by the servants. Emotions will commit mutiny, and unless you learn how to bring them back under submission, you will lose control.

Let me reiterate that this book is written unapologetically from a Christian perspective. The reason is that God has given us the ways of life and being in control, but the victory of life is only promised through a life obedient to the Lord through the word He has given.

I once had a secular editor ask me if I could write how-to articles for the secular market. In some situations, the unbeliever can glean some help from biblical principles. However, the Bible is written from the perspective of a life founded upon Christ. Limited success can be found by correcting certain behaviors, but without a solid foundation, God's principles are lacking in strength. Christ is the foundation of a solid life, and the Holy Spirit is the power which strengthens us to rise above human limitations. Without a new, Spirit-filled life, you are limited by the weakness of human nature.

The Bible refers to the failure of God's people to keep the Old Testament Law. The scripture says what the Law could not do in that it was weak through the flesh, God accomplished through His son.[19]

The flesh is weak, and anything depended upon the flesh will fall short of God's perfect plan. The Spirit of God is the power behind the Christian life. Godly principles dependent upon human effort will only have the power of the flesh. Godly principles founded upon the Spirit will have

---

[19] Romans 8:3

the power of God – and it is He who gives us His strength regardless of our weaknesses.

The overarching theme of this book is to teach you how to learn to abandon the flesh of human nature and walk in the power of God. This is how we become overcomers. It is not you becoming a better you. It is you accounting yourself as dead to the flesh and alive to God – as you were created to be.

All victory outside of God's guiding hand is a temporary illusion. If you don't think this is true, get to know someone who appears to have it all together. You'll find they have the same problems as you. Some people hide their problems from public view better than others, but all have similar struggles. Have you ever seen someone have a sudden and unexplainable meltdown? People who have always seemed so happy, in control, and blessed, sometimes have a total breakdown without warning.

It could be a nervous breakdown, unexpected divorce, or they make a foolish decision which seems so out of character. The truth is, personal problems don't suddenly arise. Problems percolate under the surface until they can be hidden no longer. The seams of life may come unraveled suddenly, but this is because something has been tearing at them for some time, and they now cannot keep it all under control.

As long as problems are small, many people can keep repairing the seams and hiding their struggles. But there are times in life when problems come too hard and too fast. Anyone can walk through a gentle stream, but let a flash flood come and even the strongest person will be swept away. That is unless they can get out of the stream.

The Bible gives us the promise that God will never give us more temptation than we can bear. He will always provide a way of escape. Temptation is not only the desire to sin, but it can be testing, trials, and anything that puts our lives to the test. God has promised to test us, but to those who trust in Him, He will not put on them more than they can bear. But what if the load we are carrying is not what God intends for us to bear? Consider **1 Peter 5:6-7**

> 6 Therefore humble yourselves under the mighty hand of God, that He may exalt you in due time,
> 7 casting all your care upon Him, for He cares for you.

What if someone refuses to cast their cares upon Him? What if temptation is the result of refusing to follow God's plan of escape? In these situations, we bear unnecessary burdens, and we must repent, or turn from our way. Part of repentance is casting our failures and weaknesses upon the Lord. We become strong, not because of our own abilities, but because we allow the Lord to bear our cares of this life.

Most of us have heard to cast our cares upon Jesus, but do we truly live under this promise? Here is the process most people follow. We start feeling emotionally taxed, so we pray for God to give us relief. We may say the words, "I'm laying this at your feet," but our heart won't let go. When problems continue to threaten, we're afraid God isn't going to handle it, so we carry the burden we claim to have laid down. As life continues to send things our way, the load grows heavier. We ask God to lift some of the weight off us, but it doesn't seem to happen. Our lives get overwhelmed and we wonder why God doesn't stop the flood.

Let's stop for a moment and look at the promise above. It begins with an important command, which leads us to the promise. The Bible is filled with promises, but we don't inherit the promises by claiming them. We inherit the promises by looking at the instructions which lead us to the promises. If we reject the instructions, we cannot lay hold of the promise.

In the above passage, we are first told to humble ourselves under the mighty hand of God. It's a twofold instruction. It is us taking the time to recognize who God is and to think upon His might. It's to recognize that God is

God and He is able to fulfill His word. And it is also an acknowledgment that He deserves our humble submission.

If I cannot humble myself and submit to the Lord, I will never see the fulfillment of His desire to lift me up. How this is done is determined by His will. He might exalt me over my stressful problems, or He may give me the power to walk victoriously in the valley of difficulty. God brings His honor through my life before the eyes of others so they can see the goodness of the Lord – not the glory of me.

As I humble myself under His mighty hand, I am putting life in its proper place. That includes my problems and cares. Pride says I have to help God carry my problems. When I recognize God is bigger than I am, and He is powerful enough to overcome my problems, I'll be willing to cast my cares upon Him. It's an act of faith.

Let's stop for a moment to examine what it means to have faith. According to the Bible, faith is believing God to the point where we put our trust in Him. We are saved by faith and nothing is of ourselves. It's the gift of God, not of works so no one can boast (Ephesians 2:8-9).

I was transformed into a new creation when I believed God's promise to forgive my sins and give me a new life in Christ. I willingly let go of my life and allowed God to take away my sins and give me an eternal life, born in the Spirit of God. I did nothing except believe and allow God to do what He promised to do.

Those who cling to their old lives don't trust God and cannot receive the new life. You may have met people like this. They say things like, "The gospel message sounds good, but I'm just not ready." They can be miserable and their lives falling apart, but they just can't let go. We also must learn to let go. Letting go of our sins so we can be forgiven is only the first step. We must also believe God has the power to not only forgive our sins and rescue our souls, but also has the power to rescue us through our daily lives.

The faith which gave us forgiveness and salvation is the same faith we live by in daily life. In the book of

Galatians, the Apostle Paul rebukes the people by saying, "Are you so foolish, having begun by faith, you now think you are perfected by the flesh?"

In other words, God transformed you by faith to create this new life in Christ. Do you now think you have to use human effort to live out the new life of God?

Do we think God can transform us into a new creation, but now He doesn't have the power to handle our problems? We must realize God's power to transform our problems into His promise, and that all things work together for the good of those who love God, and are called into His purpose.

The same faith that changed your life is how you must now live your life. How did I receive Christ and become a new person? I believed His word. He promised if I confessed Him as Lord and believed His word, He would give me the promise of salvation. It was God's work on my behalf.

How then do I cast my cares upon Him? I must believe His word. God promised that if I believe His word and humble myself under His hand, I will then have the right to cast my cares upon Him and He will not allow them to become more than I can bear. If my problems are more than I can bear, I know I'm not living in the promise.

Do you believe God?

The same holds true for overcoming my flesh and its passions. Look at the incredible promise of **Galatians 5:16-17, 24-25**

> 16 I say then: Walk in the Spirit, and you shall not fulfill the lust of the flesh.
> 17 For the flesh lusts against the Spirit, and the Spirit against the flesh; and these are contrary to one another, so that you do not do the things that you wish
> 24 And those *who are* Christ's have crucified the flesh with its passions and desires.
> 25 If we live in the Spirit, let us also walk in the Spirit.

What is the promise? If you and I walk in the Spirit, we will not fulfill the lusts of the flesh. The lust of the flesh is anything that wars against the Spirit. Anger wars against the Spirit. Guilt wars against the Spirit. Greed, envy, jealousy, lust, outbursts of wrath, hatred, bitterness, worry, anxiety and anything contrary to God wars against the Spirit. Yet we are promised if we walk in the Spirit, none of these things will be fulfilled in our lives. Even so, we struggle needlessly with all these things.

So how do we claim the promise? The same way we claimed the promise that Jesus died for our sins. God promised, you believed, and therefore, you willingly let go as God took your old life of sin and gave you a new life, born in His Spirit.

Now look at verse 24 above. You *have been* crucified with Christ. If you are Christ's, this has been done. Past tense. When you received the life of salvation, your old life was done away with. Your sins, flesh, and the passions that go along with it was crucified with Christ. Was. Not will be.

Do you believe God? If so, this promise is yours. And now you can believe and step out of the flesh and walk in the Spirit. It is a choice. If you live in the Spirit – and you do if Christ has become your Lord – you now must choose to walk in the Spirit. To choose to walk in the Spirit is not to do something to make yourself more spiritual. It is to believe God and trust in Him to take the passions away just as He took your sins away. Look to the cross where your sins were crucified. It is done, but you have the right to take the flesh up again. Taking upon us the flesh and its passions is an act of disbelief. Walking in the Spirit is an act of faith.

This is a daily realization. The Apostle Paul said, "I die daily." Our victory today will be forgotten tomorrow unless we take this step of faith. When the burden of the flesh rises up and wars against our minds, we can either submit to it, or submit under the hand of God. When I'm tempted, I must say to my flesh, "You are crucified with Christ. I believe God and therefore will walk in the Spirit."

Keep in mind that the Bible says that we are changed into Christ's likeness as we behold Him. Look to Christ and be transformed. You are a new creation. Allow God to transform your behavior from the flesh and into the new creation you now are in Christ.

It sounds simplistic, but it's life-changing. To the unredeemed, the message of the cross sounds simplistic, but it too is life-changing. In fact, there is no other way. There is no other way to salvation other than believing the word of God and surrendering to the Lord through it. There is no other way to walk victoriously in the Spirit than to believe God and submit to Him through the commands and promises He has given.

Abraham believed God and his faith was accounted to him as righteousness. From this point on he walked with God. When you believe God, it is accounted to you for righteousness. When you believe, you submit, and have the promise that sin can no longer have dominion over you. This is the promise that whom the Son sets free is free indeed.

The flesh can only rule those who submit themselves to it. It provides the illusion it has the power to subdue you, but in truth, it's a deception designed to convince you to submit back to your old life in the flesh. When it rises up, the battle is not even yours to fight. Submit to the Lord, believe the promise that your flesh – the very thing attempting to regain its former place – has been crucified with Christ.

The flesh and its passions are no longer yours. Believe God and allow Him to lead your heart. The work is the Lord's and the only thing hindering this work is your lack of submission. The flesh seeks to rule over you, but God calls for your submission by faith in Him. It's a promise that has been fulfilled and waits for you to take it.

The battle is not yours to fight.

The flesh's desire is for you, but you have the freedom to rule over it. By submitting to God, He exalts you to rule over your flesh and its passions.

# Rule or being ruled

Let me state again something I said earlier – and will probably mention again before this book concludes. Emotions, desires, and passions make good servants, but terrible masters.

When someone is driven by their passions, they have no control over life. Think about someone known for their jealousy. Do they have complete control in their life? There are times when jealous rage takes over and becomes the driving force in someone's behavior. The one with the jealousy is being driven to act out in ways that are destructive to both themselves and to other people.

A jealous man cannot trust his spouse. The passion controlling his thoughts causes him to suspect his wife of things she may not have even thought about. At least not until she is accused. Jealousy demands control. It becomes chains which strip all freedom and love from a relationship. Without trust and freedom, love can't thrive.

I used a man as the illustration, but in many women this is just as much a problem as with men. It becomes a rage within which drives the possessor to mistrust, accuse, and to lash out against those who should be loved. It becomes the problem. While this passion claims to be protecting the relationship, it is actually destroying it.

This is also true for lust, anger, bitterness, or any other thing which attempts to rise up and bring us under its rule.

God created our emotions and they serve a good purpose – as long as they remain within God's design. In fact, nothing in creation is evil by design. Everything God created in the beginning was declared by God to be *very good*. It is only when something steps outside of God's intended purpose that it becomes sinful or destructive.

The Bible says, "Be angry and do not sin." Anger is not a sin. It's an emotion designed for a purpose. When anger is mixed with sin within our fleshly desires, it becomes destructive and sinful. Most destructive anger is self-focused. When I feel offended, I get angry. When I don't get my way, I become angry. When I feel violated, I use anger to lash out at someone else. Many times our anger is not justified. We think it is, because we are measuring right and wrong based on the standard of selfishness, but in truth, selfish anger is almost always sin.

When I become angry, I will either problem solve or problem create. Problem solving is when I look at the situation that caused my anger and ask myself, what needs to be fixed? Sometimes the answer is, "Me. I need to be fixed." If I'm angry because of selfish desires, I need to find ways to reshape my thinking and attitude.

Dealing with anger should begin with an evaluation. Does the thing that angers me need to be resolved? Ninety-nine percent of the things that frustrate us are petty and not worthy of the emotional energy we put into it. Yet we allow them to strip us of peace and put us on a destructive course of action. If I stop and take time to evaluate my anger, I'll discover that sometimes the best way of solving the problem is to say, "This is petty and not worth my emotional energy," and then toss it away. When we toss it away, we are not bottling up the frustration, we are rejecting the anger and the problem as being insignificant. If it returns to my mind, I toss it out again. If something continues to dominate my thoughts, it needs to be dealt with by either putting to death my flesh, or resolving a problem.

When my reaction to a problem becomes bigger than the problem, I become the problem. The issue can't be addressed until I first resolve me. When I am under control, I can then focus on the cause of frustration.

Years ago I worked in the construction world. A coworker just returned from prison for murder. In a conversation he brought up his prison stint and explained how he murdered someone. The reason, "He disrespected me." The man made a comment which offended him, so he killed him. And he still felt justified in his actions.

This is the result of allowing our passions to be the driving force in our lives. While we may not commit crimes, self-centeredness can and will cause harm to those around us and pride blinds us to our own behaviors. Pride disguises itself in many ways – including a false sense of righteous indignation and self-justification. When life is viewed through the lens of our passions, everything will be evaluated based on how it makes us feel. Then we can't see how our actions are harming others in both big and small ways. Since we don't feel violated, we don't recognize when a problem exists.

When our lives are founded upon emotions, over-reactions to situations will become the norm, and we'll have no other method of evaluating right and wrong, other than what we feel. Or at a minimum, our feelings will trump what we know to be right and wrong. We won't even recognize our dilemma until consequences begin to arise – and even then, it's easy to justify our actions in our own minds.

Many end up blaming the consequences of their actions on others. Though people are often their own worst enemies, they can feel as though they are the victim and others are to blame.

Continuous self-evaluation is essential. And we need a standard greater than our intellect by which to evaluate our lives. This is why the Bible says, "I the Lord try the hearts. I test the mind."[20] Also, the scriptures have the power to separate our thoughts and intents of the heart and reveal our true motives.[21]

Through the scripture, the Holy Spirit judges our hearts, motives, and actions. When we have a seeking heart,

---

[20] Jeremiah 17:10
[21] Hebrews 4:12

the Lord will reveal what needs to change. We will either be Spirit led, or passion driven.

If you do not control your passions, they will control you. It's a fact. It's also something we all struggle with from time to time. Though some people are more susceptible to negative emotions than others, everyone struggles. Even though emotions are more difficult to control in some people, everyone can regain control. God has designed our minds in such a way that we can rule our feelings. The problem is we don't want to resist our urges – whether it be lust, anger, jealousy, bitterness, or any other passion. It's easy to allow ourselves to be carried, but we are called to stand firm.

I can be angry and not sin. I can overcome every negative emotion – even those which have ruled my life for years. It won't be easy, but it becomes easier as the flesh loses its dominance on our minds. The real problem is when we need self-control the most, we desire it the least. In order to have a life under control, we must value the right things, recognize the danger of the wrong things, and lay a solid foundation now.

You and I prepare for temptation now – not when we need the strength to resist.

This is why Jesus compared those who take heed to His word to the man who spent years digging into the solid foundation of rock. It was hard work, but when the storms came, he was able to stand. Those who don't do this are like the man built on sand. It's easy to stand on sand when the storms are not hammering the foundation, but when the storms come, collapse is inevitable.[22]

Now is the time to build your life on the right foundation. Unless you take heed to rebuild on the rock, your life is already built on sand.

---

[22] Matthew 7:24-27

Freedom to Rule

# Life Applications

- Memorize 1 Peter 5:6-7
- Jesus endured the cross by focusing on the joy before Him. Evaluate what you should focus on that has lasting value.
- Begin conforming your weaknesses to the likeness of Christ. Patience instead of anger, gentleness instead of outbursts, kindness instead of scorn, thankfulness instead of complaining.
- Contemplate on how these changes will benefit your life now and eternally.
- Think about the last time you blame someone else for a negative reaction. Regardless of how you feel about their actions, how can you handle your reaction in a way which submits to God so He can lift you up?
- The next time you react with a negative emotion, think about how you can submit your life and situation to God so He can lift you up.
- Think about what worries or bothers you. Pray to the Lord and put this care on Him and trust Him to resolve your heart and then resolve the problem.
- Acknowledge He has the right to use problems to refine your life and resolve problems after His will has been fulfilled in you.
- Daily take time to prayerfully die to your will and submit to walk in the Spirit. When the flesh rises up during the day, surrender to the Spirit each time.
- Take time to review Life Applications from other chapters.

# Forgiveness

This topic will be the lengthiest section of this book, so I'm breaking it into two chapters. There is so much we need to understand about forgiveness that it is necessary to cover this topic more fully. All of God's commands are intended for our good, but few commands produce immediate results like the command to forgive. Yes, forgiveness is a command – not an option.

Let's first look at the results of unforgiveness. Harboring resentment and anger creates more stress on our minds than any other cause. It's like a weight than we never put down. We might endure the stress of carrying this burden, but we'll never thrive as we could. The longer we carry it, the more blind we are to its presence in our lives. This is why childhood traumas have such lasting impacts. Long after we've forgotten the specifics, we struggle with the symptoms.

Victims of bitterness often don't even know why they are bitter. Or why they have certain emotional scars. It becomes part of our personalities and what drives many of our emotional reactions.

Anger and unforgiveness creates bitterness and hatred. Everyone is wronged. Any person who lives among other people will be offended and done wrong. Human nature cannot be removed from our social world. This is even true in church. Sometimes it appears that offenses are more common in churches, but this is because relationships are more intimate in a congregation, and the opportunity to offend becomes greater.

You will be wronged. You may not realize it, but you will also wrong other people. Sometimes one comment, a slip of the tongue, can create a chain of events with consequences we could have never anticipated. Churches split, families divide, friends become enemies – all from one misspoken word which hit an area of sensitivity in another person. Children fight and make up, but adult disputes can last a lifetime. This problem has always existed and we must learn to deal with it. Consider the words of **James 3:2, 5-10**

> 2 For we all stumble in many things. If anyone does not stumble in word, he *is* a perfect man, able also to bridle the whole body.
>
> ...
>
> 5 Even so the tongue is a little member and boasts great things. See how great a forest a little fire kindles!
>
> 6 And the tongue *is* a fire, a world of iniquity. The tongue is so set among our members that it defiles the whole body, and sets on fire the course of nature; and it is set on fire by hell.
>
> 7 For every kind of beast and bird, of reptile and creature of the sea, is tamed and has been tamed by mankind.
>
> 8 But no man can tame the tongue. *It is* an unruly evil, full of deadly poison.
>
> 9 With it we bless our God and Father, and with it we curse men, who have been made in the similitude of God.
>
> 10 Out of the same mouth proceed blessing and cursing. My brethren, these things ought not to be so.

Let's first take note of how James introduces this discussion. If anyone doesn't stumble in their words, they would be a perfect person. Keep in mind, this applies to all. As mentioned earlier, when the Bible uses the word 'man' in the general sense, it is referring to mankind – both men and women.

Who doesn't slip up with their words and say things that offend? No one. Everyone struggles to control their tongue – this includes you and I. Our words are compared to a match in a forest. Sometimes one word can cause a fire that spreads outward and causes much unexpected damage.

We say things thoughtlessly that can create a firestorm, but we also say things spitefully. As James puts it, the same mouth which praises God is a curse to man. These things ought not to be, but they are. James is speaking to the church. Though we should be guarding our mouths, in a moment of carelessness or a moment of anger, we say things which have serious consequences.

Saying, "I shouldn't have said that," doesn't stop the fire. Someone once shared this illustration I believe is fitting. A man took his kids in the bathroom and squeezed all the toothpaste into a sink. He offered ten dollars to the first child who could put the toothpaste back into the tube. Some tried, but no one had success. He then said, "This is what happens with your words. Once they're out of your mouth, you can't put them back in."

King Solomon put it this way, "Death and life are in the power of the tongue." Sometimes our words are life to the hearers. A word of praise. A word of encouragement. A kind gesture.

Other times our words are death. Discouragement, carelessness toward someone's feelings, statements that drive right to the heart of another, these can all be daggers to the soul of the hearer. Instead of bearing up those who are weak, we have a tendency to say things that add to their burden and shatter the emotions of those around us. Because we struggle with our own sinful flesh, we have a tendency to speak more words which kill the emotions of others than we use words that give life and encouragement.

I say all of this to make an important point. You are guilty. So am I. We will say things which ought not to come from our mouths. We offend and then expect others to not take offense. Yet we then want to hold them to a higher standard than we are willing to hold ourselves. I've seen people apologize and be rejected. "I can never forget what you said," the offended person says.

If we were held in contempt for every word spoken, the wars would never end. For some people they don't. For many, it's a silent war. In churches and families the cold war rages in a never ending standoff.

Think for a moment on our own ways of dealing with words. Have you ever been offended and had someone say something like, "What did I say?" Or perhaps we've asked the same question. Someone comes up to us a week or a month later and says, "You hurt me by what you said." Immediately we rack our brains thinking, *What could I have said? I don't remember saying something offensive.*

We live in a self-centered perspective. When I speak, I'm evaluating my conversations based on what I feel and what I have experienced. There are times when people are offended at something that seems ridiculous to me. I can't see their feelings. I can't know their experiences. I don't know what is fragile in their emotional makeup, so an offense won't make sense to me.

The opposite is also true. What cuts me deeply may seem like a passing comment to the other person. They aren't bothered, so why am I? They don't know I'm sensitive about the way I look, or the way I talk, or that I feel insecure because I can't afford nicer clothes. They don't know I don't feel accepted when they mention 'those people on that side of the tracks.'

We all offend. We all get offended. It's how we respond that affects our lives. It's true that we should always seek reconciliation and give a heartfelt apology when we've offended others. However, this book is going to focus on how we deal with forgiving those who will never apologize. People will offend and not be able to see the wrong they have done.

There are people who don't care if they have offended us. There are people who are abusive. There are even people who take pleasure in hurting others. There are also those who cannot see how their actions or words are harmful to others. These will not apologize and if not handled properly, it leaves an open wound. Open wounds don't heal. But learning the true meaning of forgiveness is the salve that heals.

We learn to handle the offenses of others by learning how to deal with ourselves. The solution is not to change others. You can't change the other person. You and I must learn how to deal with offenses in a healthy manner while also learning how to take care not to be the cause of offense. It is our responsibility, regardless of who has the greater fault.

# A personal testimony.

Let me tell a true-life experience that taught me much about forgiveness. Several years ago I worked as an IT professional. I loved the type of work I did and my performance showed it. I was promoted several times and eventually became the team lead for our department. The company I worked for had some financial struggles and was hit hard by layoffs. Our team was cut in half and we were merged with another technical team. My manager didn't survive the cuts so I now reported to the other team's manager.

I already knew this manager and quickly established a good working relationship. Then one day I was asked to do something unethical. I won't go into details, but it was something commonly practiced by my new team in order to falsify performance reporting. When I brought up the discrepancy to my manager, the reaction was immediate and harsh. I was demoted from a lead position and my manager made the comment, "When I right someone off, I never go back and I never forgive."

No truer words were ever spoken. What I thought had been an honest mistake turned out to be the way the team hid unethical practices. For the next three years my manager did everything within his/her power to destroy me. I was given impossible projects that required 70-80 hours a week to accomplish. Being salaried, there was no extra pay.

When I completed the project, it would be transferred to someone else so I didn't get credit. The reason for the change, "Eddie wasn't able to get the job done, so I transferred it to Bob from Account Temps." Never mind that the work had already been completed.

I was given work in two cities that were due at the same time. One would inevitably go past due. My manager also put me in charge of the parts room. When I was sent to a different state to work, I was still responsible for issuing and watching over the inventory of parts in my home state. My inability to get back in time to issue parts to other technicians was noted as a failure on my performance review, but not the reason why.

To make a long story shorter, anything that could be done to show me in a bad light was done. On my yearly performance review, I was given an unsatisfactory rating and dozens of infractions were listed against me. Knowing this was coming, I logged every email, communication, and job. I disputed my review and provided a thirty-page document detailing every perceived infraction, and proving why the accusations were false. Human Resources (HR) complimented me on the details of my documentation and removed every infraction from my record, but they refused to remove the poor performance rating.

I was frustrated. I was a salaried employee, so I got no overtime, but I had more than double the workload of anyone else on the team. To keep up I put in up to thirty hours a week unpaid overtime. Sometimes forty. I mapped out my coverage area – forty-thousand square miles. The next closest person had one hundred square miles.

When I left in the morning, my kids were asleep. When I came home, my kids were asleep. I looked for another job, but with five kids I couldn't afford a pay cut, and the economy wasn't offering many positions at my level. I was growing bitter, grumpy, and miserable. I kept praying, "Lord, why are you letting this happen? Get me out of this situation." When I applied for jobs within the company, my manager would give a bad report and nix my chances.

Another year rolled by and it was time for my next annual performance review. I knew what was coming. It would be another substandard performance review. The previous year I had disputed the slander and every allegation was proven false. My complaint was noted, but the manager had an explanation that apparently persuaded HR not to act. Now I was in the same position again. Do I dispute? Last year it did no good, created more tension, plus it was stressful trying to present my case to a skeptical corporate Human Resources department – a group that naturally wanted to support management.

While I pondered my difficult situation, I prayed for guidance. In my morning devotion, I came across this passage in **1 Peter 2:23**

When He was reviled, did not revile in return; when
He suffered, He did not threaten, but committed
*Himself* to Him who judges righteously;

It didn't make much of an impression on my heavy mind at the time. I headed out for the long drive and listened to my Bible on audio. My audio was at 1 Peter and I heard this passage again. What a coincidence. Later in the day, I was driving between sites and turned on the radio. Just as the radio came on, someone was reading scripture for a sermon, "When He was reviled, did not revile in return...but committed Himself to Him who judges righteously."

I turned off the radio. *Three times in one day. Lord, are you trying to show me something?*

I began praying for God to open my eyes to see what He was showing me. That's a prayer God quickly answered. I couldn't see it before because I had only been focused on my own misery. My focus was on the wrongs being done, not on the work God wanted to do.

It was like blinders fell from my eyes and the bigger picture of God's plan unfolded in my mind's eye. This was a refining process. I had seen God work in my life through the good things and the situations I understood were blessings, but I didn't recognize the true blessing of God refining my life and showing me what was truly important.

My job wasn't something I had control over. Nor did I need to fret over it. If it was truly a blessing from God, it was God who gave it, and only God who could take it away. This manager could rage against me, but had no power beyond what God was willing to put me through. And according to scripture, if I'm walking in God's purposes, everything works toward my good.

Did I believe this was true? I knew it was.

Suddenly I felt a load lifted off my shoulders.

Then God hit me with something I wasn't sure I could do. Rather than me telling you, let's look at the scripture's command in **Matthew 18:23-35**

> 23 "Therefore the kingdom of heaven is like a certain king who wanted to settle accounts with his servants.
>
> 24 "And when he had begun to settle accounts, one was brought to him who owed him ten thousand talents.
>
> 25 "But as he was not able to pay, his master commanded that he be sold, with his wife and children and all that he had, and that payment be made.
>
> 26 "The servant therefore fell down before him, saying, 'Master, have patience with me, and I will pay you all.'
>
> 27 "Then the master of that servant was moved with compassion, released him, and forgave him the debt.
>
> 28 "But that servant went out and found one of his fellow servants who owed him a hundred denarii; and he laid hands on him and took *him* by the throat, saying, 'Pay me what you owe!'

²⁹ "So his fellow servant fell down at his feet and begged him, saying, 'Have patience with me, and I will pay you all.'

³⁰ "And he would not, but went and threw him into prison till he should pay the debt.

³¹ "So when his fellow servants saw what had been done, they were very grieved, and came and told their master all that had been done.

³² "Then his master, after he had called him, said to him, 'You wicked servant! I forgave you all that debt because you begged me.

³³ 'Should you not also have had compassion on your fellow servant, just as I had pity on you?'

³⁴ "And his master was angry, and delivered him to the torturers until he should pay all that was due to him.

³⁵ "So My heavenly Father also will do to you if each of you, from his heart, does not forgive his brother his trespasses."

God was not only teaching me patience and trust, but He was teaching me what it truly means to forgive.

One thing we must realize is that sin is a debt. When I sin, that sin must be paid. The Bible says every sin will be held in account before God. For us as Christians, our debt has been paid, for Jesus bore that debt upon the cross. That's why Jesus said in the model prayer, "Forgive us of our debts as we forgive our debtors."

My manager was a debtor to me. Every wrong was piling up in the account I was keeping track of. Even subconsciously, we keep a mental note of wrongs and recount them when something reminds us. Jesus' disciple, Peter, made a statement he thought was a noble effort. "How many times should we forgive someone? Seven times?"

Seven was a generous offer by human standards. Freely forgiving seven times is more than most people would do. Most times it only takes one offense to create an enemy.

Jesus' answer took the records of debt away completely. "Not until seven times, but seventy times seven." Four-hundred and ninety times. You see, I can remember seven times, but there is no way I can keep track of four-hundred and ninety. Even if I forgive from the heart, my memory can go back seven times. But Jesus pushed the number beyond our ability to remember. In other words, never stop forgiving. If I'm keeping records, I have failed to forgive. When I remember the wrong, I am commanded to erase it again.

As a self-protection method, I had been keeping track of my manager's wrongs. I could easily have produced another thirty-page defense. I could have produced a hundred-page defense. But the Lord shattered my rationale. I thought about my record keeping and remembered, seventy times seven.

When I'm keeping records, I am taking my problems out of God's hands and setting myself up as the debt holder. Which also puts me under the debt, for I have decided to be judged under a human standard instead of by grace.

Don't misunderstand what is being said. The passage of the unforgiving servant is not referring to salvation. All our sins have been paid by Christ and will not be held against us again. Jesus was speaking to people who were under the Old Covenant. We are under the New Covenant that is dependent upon Christ and not based on our performance or ability to keep the law. However, there is a truth that applies to us as well.

The scriptures teach that even the Christian will be judged for what is done in the body. This is not the Lord measuring our good against our bad, but are we in the Spirit or in the flesh. An unforgiving Christian is placing themselves into the flesh where sin reigns. I cannot be in the Spirit if I am in the flesh. Therefore, if I try to live by the Old Covenant, I am abiding in the flesh and can never earn enough forgiveness points to emerge from my debt.

The unforgiving Christian has chosen to live according to the flesh and will never be able to walk in the Spirit until they let go of unforgiveness. They are choosing to walk under the Old Covenant, where the flesh is measured based on its weakness and not by grace. Grace is still given, but I cannot walk according to God's grace while demanding to reign over others in the flesh.

Did I want God to be in control, or me? At this point, I had a two-year track record. None of my work and recordkeeping had done much good. Easy choice on that one.

*But look how many things this person has done to me*, I thought – wanting to justify my anger. Then I remembered the passage above. I was the man with more debt than he could pay. Did I want to measure life according to a fleshly standard, or did I want to experience the fullness of grace?

To put Jesus' parable into perspective, the man who owed ten-thousand talents could never pay it. It's ironic that he pled, "Have mercy and I will pay all." The only thing the Lord listened to was, "Have mercy on me." The debtor could never have paid it all. A talent was a weight of measure which is approximately 130 pounds. In this scenario, it was gold measured out by weight. What would a hundred and thirty pounds of gold cost in today's market? Now multiply that by ten-thousand. I don't think a man who was penniless would have any hope of repaying one talent, much less ten-thousand gold talents.

A day's wage in that era was a denarii. His fellow who owed him 100 denarii did have a significant debt. It would take one-hundred days of labor to pay the man back. But what is that in comparison to the billions of day's wages he owed, but had been forgiven?

The picture Jesus is painting regarding forgiveness is that you can never repay God for the offense you have done. Or I have done. Every sinful thought, action, lie, offense, and wrong is a debt we cannot repay. The flesh can never produce good, so even a lifetime of servitude cannot repay anything to God.

Jesus even took sin to the reality of the human heart when He said, "I say to you that anyone who looks at a woman to lust has already committed adultery in his heart." Think about this the next time you do a double take when an attractive man or woman walks by. He said greed is equal to thievery, envy equals idolatry, hatred is murder, etc. There is no limit to the debt I have to God. Yet He forgave me of all that debt, and now He is asking me to release the debt of wrongs done to me. God offers grace freely, but I have the right to ignore grace and hold on to the flesh.

I tossed aside my records. But that wasn't enough. It's not to just ignore the wrongs done; it was to forgive them from the heart. And what is the evidence of forgiveness? Remember the first verse we looked at? God has given us power, love, and a sound mind. Forgiveness flows out of that love and is something God has empowered us with the ability to do. Look now at **Matthew 5:44-46**

44 But I say to you, love your enemies, bless those who curse you, do good to those who hate you, and pray for those who spitefully use you and persecute you,

45 that you may be sons of your Father in heaven; for He makes His sun rise on the evil and on the good, and sends rain on the just and on the unjust.

46 For if you love those who love you, what reward have you? Do not even the tax collectors do the same?

This is forgiveness in action. It's hard to do, but necessary. Until I forgive, bitterness and hatred remain. Bitterness and hatred don't only destroy the person they are against, these also destroy the one who possesses them. Did I want to forfeit my reward in order to hold onto debt?

Have you ever seen a hateful person who has joy? Are they happy? Bitterness is the bars of our own prison cell. It becomes a prison we construct to confine ourselves in order to get back at our enemy.

Love your enemies. How do I do that? According to Jesus, I must bless. I must do good. I must pray for them. Pray for, not against. "God, get them back for me," is not praying for our enemies. "Lord, I release them of all wrong. Bless them, forgive them, and give me an opportunity to do good for them," is a prayer of forgiveness.

It isn't for you or I to judge someone's worthiness of forgiveness. God's first desire is always mercy. It's God's desire for your enemy to repent of their wrongs, surrender to God's mercy, and find forgiveness through Christ. This makes your enemy a brother or sister in Christ. Just as those whom you have wronged have no right to demand God refuse mercy to you, you have no right to demand for God to be merciless to another person.

Is forgiveness hard? You bet it is. And it takes time to heal. But this healing is applied each time we forgive. When our mind conjures up past wrongs, it's a reminder to pray for that person. You'll find deliverance from your own pain when you deliver that person from debt. Your pain will remind you of that person, and this should remind you of the command to forgive, pray, and seek their good. When you do so, there is a reward. Look at **Proverbs 25:21-22**

21 If your enemy is hungry, give him bread to eat;
And if he is thirsty, give him water to drink;
22 For *so* you will heap coals of fire on his head, And the LORD will reward you.

The Lord rewards those who follow His word. Your first reward is peace and deliverance from anger and bitterness. Also, when we forgive, we are placing ourselves in the center of God's grace for our own lives.

The choices are to remain angry, become bitter, refuse God's will for our own life, and suffer the consequences. Bitterness is the most destructive force in your emotions. Clinging to it is like poisoning your mind. Yet our human nature would rather poison itself than release the debt of another. But God has given us the power to act according to our new nature in Christ.

After you forgive, the wrongs will come to mind again. And again. And again. You have trained your thought patterns to dwell on the things that bother you. Now you have to change your way of thinking. And this doesn't come easy.

After God revealed these things to me, the relief was almost overwhelming. No longer was I controlled by my enemy, but I found a peace that had evaded me for two years. As I thought upon these things and began to see how much it caused me to grow spiritually and emotionally, I would have written a 'thank you letter' if I didn't think it would have antagonized the situation.

Then something happened. A new wave of attacks came. Though I had forgiven and felt such sweet relief, all my anger and frustration came pouring back when the next wrong came along. I had to wrestle with my emotions again. I had to go through the forgiveness process again. I had to make myself say the words, "I forgive you," and then pray for that person's good. I had to wrestle with my heart so I could sincerely bless that person. Over time I learned how to do this better, but it was never easy to forgive someone I knew would never even acknowledge the wrong. In the end, who is better off? The person saying, "I forgive you and I bless you?" Or the one seething with hatred and trying to find a way to cause more harm?

While my manager was in bondage by the vindictive attitude controlling them, the attacks became my blessing.

It would be another year before God removed me from this situation. On occasions I remember this manager and pray for them. The wrongs I suffered can never be undone, but the Lord rewards and out-blesses any wrong.

# Life Applications

- Memorize Matthew 5:44-45
- Memorize Proverbs 24:17-18
- Pick out an offense or someone who has hurt you. Say out loud, "I forgive you." Consciously release that person of their debt against you.
- If you have hard feelings against anyone, take time out and pray for that person.
  - Pray for God to forgive them.
  - Pray for God to reveal His mercy to them.
  - Pray for God to bless them.
- Continue going through any offenses or hurtful relationships and forgive, then pray for the person who has caused you pain.
- Each time you feel hurt or remember a wrong done, follow the above steps to forgive and pray for the person who wronged you. Don't allow your feelings to fester.
- Review Life Applications from previous chapters.

# Is Unforgiveness ever Justified?

When the topic of forgiveness comes up, people often ask, "What if the other person refuses to apologize? Do I still have to forgive them?" Sometimes people wrong us but are not sorry. The Bible says if someone asks for forgiveness we must forgive, but what if they are not repentant?

This is a good question and is something every person will have to deal with throughout their life. I've touched on this a bit from my life's experience, but since letting go of wrongs can be difficult, we need to look at this question from a biblical perspective as well. When we stop and look at it from a wider perspective, I'm confident you'll see why it's necessary to forgive – period. We can't hold those who wrong us to a higher standard than we want to be held to. Jesus addressed this concept in **Matthew 7:1-2**

1 "Judge not, that you be not judged.

2 "For with what judgment you judge, you will be judged; and with the measure you use, it will be measured back to you.

This is not saying we shouldn't use good judgment or evaluate right from wrong, but that we must judge based on the standard we are willing to stand upon. How many unconfessed sins have I committed in my life? Wrong thoughts, selfish motives, words of offense to others, or any number of other things. We are all guilty. Do we want to judge ourselves for our unconfessed transgressions? Do we want to live under the burden of the Old Covenant?

If I want to live under the law, I cannot experience the fullness of grace. Not only can I not measure up to God's standard by my own performance, I also cannot demand someone else to measure up to performance based righteousness. Can I expect to walk in the joy of God's grace while demanding others to fulfill the law? Is this not what God is addressing in **Romans 2:1-8**

¹ Therefore you are inexcusable, O man, whoever you are who judge, for in whatever you judge another you condemn yourself; for you who judge practice the same things.

² But we know that the judgment of God is according to truth against those who practice such things.

³ And do you think this, O man, you who judge those practicing such things, and doing the same, that you will escape the judgment of God?

⁴ Or do you despise the riches of His goodness, forbearance, and longsuffering, not knowing that the goodness of God leads you to repentance?

⁵ But in accordance with your hardness and your impenitent heart you are treasuring up for yourself wrath in the day of wrath and revelation of the righteous judgment of God,

⁶ who "will render to each one according to his deeds":

⁷ eternal life to those who by patient continuance in doing good seek for glory, honor, and immortality;

⁸ but to those who are self-seeking and do not obey the truth, but obey unrighteousness -- indignation and wrath,

Think about the weight of this passage. Those who judge are condemning themselves, for they are doing the same things. When we judge someone else unworthy of forgiveness, we are also judging ourselves unworthy, for we do the same things. When I refuse to forgive, I am despising the goodness of God. Though I may think I am holding my neighbor accountable, in truth I'm rejecting God's grace and demanding to live under the law. I am the judge against my own behaviors.

My judgment is not because God was unwilling to forgive, but because I was unwilling to forgive. Instead of storing up for myself the treasures of heaven, I am storing up for myself judgment by which I will stand before God to answer for my guilt. And I will be my own condemner as God allows me to judge myself by the standard I have demanded.

As stated before, this is not the loss of salvation, but the forfeiture of my rewards and inheritance. I cannot inherit from the law, for the law and any works done under human standards will not survive the judgment seat of Christ. See 2 Corinthians 5:10 and 1 Corinthians 3:11-15.

Anyone who doesn't recognize their own sin is blind, prideful, and still in their sins. If I think I'm guiltless, I'm a fool. How many times have I said thoughtless things to my wife, kids, or those around me? Sometimes I don't even realize I have done this. Other times I have realized it, but just didn't think it was a big enough deal to address it. If they didn't say anything, I assume it didn't bother them. But often they are wounded in silence. Can I now declare my neighbor guilty because he or she failed to apologize to me? If I do, then I am now holding myself to that same works-based religious standard.

What about our hidden sins? As we have seen, Jesus said, any who have ever looked upon someone to lust after them has committed adultery in their heart. Any who are greedy are thieves. Those who are covetous are idolaters. Those who hate are murderers. My life consistently fails to stand up to God's requirement of perfection. But in the grace of God given through Christ, I am forgiven and I walk in newness of life. Yet, I have not combed through my past and confessed every sin. That's impossible. It is my life that has repented and everything is taken out of the way when I look to the cross.

Yet Jesus warned His disciples that if they hold their neighbor accountable and demand judgment, they are living according to the legal standards of the Law. The law has no mercy, it only condemns. But we are not under the law. We are under grace. And now we have the command to love from the perspective of grace.

So the argument of some is that the story of Jesus and the wicked servant is how the man asked for forgiveness and was denied. While this is true, it isn't the point of the parable. The point of the parable is that we stand upon grace and God requires us to love others with the love He has given to us.

No exceptions are given. He didn't say the onus is on our brother to ask. The onus is on us to forgive from our heart – not based on our brother's worthiness, but based on God's abundant mercies shown to us. God is not required to honor any loophole we think we can find in His word. The issue is we must forgive from the heart, not out of obligation once a set of rules has satisfied us.

The servant held his neighbor to a higher standard than God held him to. So if someone wants to hold their neighbor accountable for unconfessed wrongs, fine. They should be aware that they are placing themselves under the same standard of law. Under that standard, they must go through every minute of their lives and identify every sin they have ever committed. They must then confess them to God and find the person wronged or they thought evil toward, and confess to them. This isn't only actions, but thoughts, sins of omissions, words, and even wicked emotions such as lust, jealousy, covetousness, envy, hatred, and unjustified anger.

To demand this method of religion is utterly foolish. A person under this system will never have joy, never have peace, never have unity, and will never experience intimacy with God. God forgives, shows mercy, and pours out His grace through the Spirit. But that can't be experienced by the one who lives according to the law. That person is still in the flesh and not in the Spirit.

Hopefully you can see the value of forgiveness. Not only does God show you mercy, but God empowers you to rise above your harmful emotions and strengthens you to forgive. When you forgive, anger will attempt to rise up again, but you must cast it out. Look to the Lord for strength and refuse to allow anger, hatred, and bitterness to rule over you. Forgive, bless, pray for, and do good to those who have wronged you, and the Lord will reward you.

This is God's desire – to reward you. One of the greatest rewards is the peace of God which will reign in your heart, but this isn't where the reward ends. Forgiveness releases you from the harmful emotions which rule you, so forgiveness is just as much an act of God's mercy toward you as it is of your mercy toward another – and more so.

When you forgive, you are putting yourself in a right relationship with God and stepping onto the path of God's purpose for your life. Forgiveness is a giant leap toward peace and joy. Forgiveness is not only a commandment, but it is necessary for your own emotional and physical health.

# Examine Yourself.

We've looked at the reasons why forgiveness is necessary, but it's also important to examine ourselves and see if there is anyone we need to forgive. Begin now and search your past. When you think of someone, does your stomach tighten or your heart ache?

Ideally, we want reconciliation; however, this is not always possible. It takes two to reconcile, but only takes your willing heart to step into a life of forgiveness. Do you need to forgive a parent, relative, betrayal of a friend, or the harm caused by a stranger? Remember, God has promised healing and blessings to those who forgive. It won't be easy, but the rewards are great.

When we refuse to forgive, we give our enemies or those who have wronged us power over our emotions, and ultimately our lives. Forgiveness takes the burden off our hearts and places it on God's shoulders, where it belongs.

Don't lose sight of the example of Christ. Though He was betrayed by a close friend, rejected by His own people, tried for a crime He didn't commit, and executed by a

Roman governor who testified, "I find no wrong in this man," He forgave.

On the cross Christ declared, "Father, forgive them for they don't know what they do." They knew what they were doing to Him, but they were blinded by human nature. Foolishly, they allowed their own misguided ideas to drive their emotions into hatred. Then all they could see was that Jesus was a threat to their desires and personal beliefs. Their understanding did not go beyond the quest for self-fulfillment.

Some of the very people who demanded Jesus' death later came to faith in Christ and found God's mercies. Though Christ was persecuted and reviled, He didn't lash back in return. He committed Himself to the Father, who judges righteously. And what does our Heavenly Father desire most? Reconciliation and forgiveness.

When we commit the wrongs against us to our Heavenly Father, it is an act of faith. We are acknowledging our own need and are recognizing God has the right to show mercy to those who have wronged us – just as He reconciled us, who have wronged Him.

Don't forget that a single sin separates us from our God, for all sin is a challenge to His right to require His creation to live according to His character and nature. We are created in God's image, but we fall short of this standard when we turn from God and choose our own ways. Since one sin causes us to fall away from God's image and perfection, reconciliation must go through the cross. On the cross, Jesus was credited with our sins so we could be credited with His righteousness (2 Corinthians 5:21).

This means any sin you or I commit is responsible for putting Christ on the cross. We are responsible for His suffering and death; therefore, what wrong can we endure that is greater than condemning Jesus and putting Him to death on the cross?

Forgiveness is an act of faith because we are putting our trust in God to handle the situation according to His own wisdom. It's saying, "God I trust you to make this situation right. I can only see this from my limited perspective, but you see the good you're going to bring through this."

In the Old Testament, Joseph's brothers hated him with such passion that they could not say a peaceable word to him. They wanted to murder him, but when they saw a band of traders passing by, they decided it would be better to make a little money off him, so they sold him as a slave. They coldly ignored his anguished cries and rejoiced that the brother they hated was gone. Heartlessly, they conjured up a story to make their father believe Joseph had been killed by a wild animal. Grief almost destroyed their father, but they held to their story.

In the end, God blessed Joseph and exalted him to become the governor of Egypt. In hindsight, we see God was preparing the way for Joseph's family to be delivered from a coming famine. When all things were concluded, Joseph was in a position of authority and could have brought vengeance down on his brothers. Instead he looked at the plan of God and said, "You meant this for harm, but God meant it for good."

The Lord used the hate of Joseph's brothers as a tool to test Joseph, shape his character, and then bless his life in ways that would not have been possible if he had stayed in the safety of his home. But one important thing to note is Joseph's forgiveness. He acknowledged the wrong, but then credited it to God. It was something God not only allowed, but He orchestrated these events so Joseph could ultimately find the goodness of the Lord, and be in a spiritual condition to receive it. He forgave his brothers and became a blessing to them.

Joseph forgave because he took his eyes off the wrong and looked to God's plan. By looking at the bigger picture of God's plan, Joseph could see the hand of God through the hardships, pain, and then through his exaltation. If his anger had bound him to the wrongs done, Joseph would have been blind to the work of God. He would have then fought against God's plan instead of being an instrument of blessing.

Could God have used Joseph if he hadn't trusted the Lord enough to forgive?

Knowing Joseph was in a position where he could now retaliate, his brothers were living in fear, but Joseph spoke kindly to them. "Fear not," he said. "Though you meant it for evil, God meant it for good. It was necessary to save the lives of many. I will take care of you and nourish you and your families."

At no time in Joseph's life do you see bitterness. In fact, his positive attitude caused him to find favor in each situation – including several years when he was wrongfully in prison.

Forgiveness is also an acknowledgement of our need. I need forgiveness. I need God's mercies. I recognize I'm not upright in all my ways. I want to be, but I fall short. Because I recognize my need, I also recognize the importance of not holding others to a standard I don't want applied to my own life. Forgiveness is an acknowledgement of God's mercy over me. I forgive because I have been forgiven.

Unforgiveness reveals the opposite. When I refuse to forgive, I am declaring that I don't recognize my own need, and therefore do not acknowledge the greatness of God's mercy and grace toward me.

Unforgiveness is my declaration that God doesn't have the right to put me through hardships in order to use me to be an instrument of blessing in His miraculous plan. It is to say my temporary comfort is more valuable than God's eternal plan. It is to say, I'd rather have short-term comfort than be patient enough to see the salvation of the Lord – and have the blessing of being part of that salvation.

I cannot plead for mercy in my own life and then demand justice in the life of others. Consider **James 2:13**

For judgment is without mercy to the one who has shown no mercy. Mercy triumphs over judgment.

What a beautiful passage! Mercy triumphs over judgment. When you and I forgive, we are showing mercy. The other person has committed a wrong and is indebted to me – whether they realize it or not. But because I have been shown mercy and God forgave me all that debt, I recognize the necessity to show God's mercy to others.

This is what Jesus was saying in the parable about the two servants. The one with so great a debt couldn't see his own need.

Instead of holding our grudge as a demand for payment for a wrong, we release it to the Lord, trusting in His mercies – both to us, and to the one we are forgiving. Not only are you setting that person free, but you are setting yourself free as well. The cage of bitterness opens and you walk out. Then you are free from the chains of bitterness and your debt has now been overcome by mercy.

Let me reiterate what was stated in the last chapter. Forgiveness is essential for emotional, spiritual, and often for physical health.

# Life Applications

- Memorize Matthew 7:1-2
- Think about something in your life God forgave you of. Thank God for showing mercy.
- Read Isaiah 14:12-15.
- Read Proverbs 16:18
- Read James 4:6-8
- What was the cause of Satan's (Lucifer's) fall?
- How does pride blind us to our own destructive behaviors?
- Think upon the ways that pride interferes with your obedience to God.
- Think about how pride prevents us from forgiving.
- Repent – or turn from – your own pride, confess this sin to God, and pray for a willing heart to forgive others.
- Submit to God that you may experience the power to resist temptation – including pride.

# A Blessed Confidence

Stop trusting in man, who has but a breath in his
nostrils. Of what account is he?
**Isaiah 2:22** NIV

When Jesus began His ministry, He performed
miracles that caused many to believe on Him. But the Bible
says even though the people were praising Him, Jesus didn't
commit Himself to them, for He knew what was in man.[23]

People are fickle. In a short moment a friend can
become a foe. In Jesus' life, one day the masses were
shouting, "Hosanna, blessed is He who comes in the name of
the Lord," and a few short days later, the same crowd was
crying, "Crucify Him!"

We cannot make people into our confidence. There are
indeed loyal friends and faithful spouses; however, even a
true companion does not have the capacity to bear the
burden of our happiness. It's unjust to put the weight of
your emotional health on the shoulders of another. It's also
a recipe for your own disaster.

People aren't perfect and they will let you down. You
will also let them down. Each of us views the world from our
own perspective and what makes me happy may not make
my wife or friends happy. Add to that, if I am burdening
those around me with the demands of my own perceived
needs, I am also driving love out of those relationships.

Human nature falsely identifies love as a relationship
that meets the individual's perceived needs. I'm using the
term 'perceived needs' because many times what we think is
a need, or what we think will provide fulfillment, is based
on our perception at the moment. Perceived needs often
drive people to seek fulfillment in ways that may or may not
be healthy. What is a perceived need today may not be
something we value tomorrow.

---

[23] John 2:22-25

When we look at relationships based on what will make us happy, we aren't truly seeking love, but self. Selfish motives are often misinterpreted as love, but love is much deeper and stronger than self-serving motives. Let's take a moment to consider the meaning of love. We'll turn to the scriptures for a perfect definition. **1 Corinthians 13:4-7**

4 Love suffers long *and* is kind; love does not envy; love does not parade itself, is not puffed up;

5 does not behave rudely, does not seek its own, is not provoked, thinks no evil;

6 does not rejoice in iniquity, but rejoices in the truth;

7 bears all things, believes all things, hopes all things, endures all things.

I want to zero in on the core of love found in verse 5 – "Love does not seek its own." I listened to a young woman explain why she loved her fiancé, "I love him because he makes me happy."

True love is outward focused, not inward focused. What happens when he doesn't make you happy? What happens when the beauty fades from the youth of the bride? What happens when the strong, handsome man becomes balding and middle-aged? There is a selfish love and there is a true (or Agape) love. Self-love seeks its own, but true love seeks to give to another.

When I am dependent upon my spouse for happiness, my love becomes dependent upon her ability to meet my perceived needs. When she is dependent upon me, her love is dependent upon what I can do for her. Self-love eventually becomes two people taking from each other, and then resenting one another when needs are not met. True love does not seek its own, but seeks the good of another person.

When both sides understand true God-given love, it becomes two people giving to each other and finding fulfillment through benefiting the other.

When giving love is the focus, love endures all things, is not provoked into resentment, and doesn't rejoice in iniquity. True love will never rejoice in doing something to avenge a wrong on the other person. That can be active aggression, or passive aggression. Passive aggression is doing or saying little things we know will hurt the other in small ways, while pretending not to be the aggressor. Any time I am giving into the desire to retaliate in any way, I have stepped outside of love.

God has given us the checks and balances to examine our lives to see if we are truly walking in love. Let's again be reminded of this book's overarching passage – God has given us power, love, and a sound mind. Love comes from the Lord and as we submit to His word, we discover how to walk in the outpouring of His love.

There's an important truth often overlooked and most people never learn about relationships. I believe this passage from **Jeremiah 17:5-10** explains it well:

> [5] Thus says the LORD: "Cursed *is* the man who trusts in man And makes flesh his strength, Whose heart departs from the LORD.
> [6] For he shall be like a shrub in the desert, And shall not see when good comes, But shall inhabit the parched places in the wilderness, *In* a salt land *which is* not inhabited.

Let's pause before going on and reflect on what is being said. Relationships can be a curse if we put our trust in a person or group of people. My trust may also be in my own abilities or possessions. This is what is meant by making flesh our strength. Mankind is not our provider. Even if there is a dependence upon another person, it is still God's provision. My job is the means by which God blesses me to take care of the physical needs of my family. Though the channel by which our financial needs are met may be through my employer, the employer is not my provider. Employers can turn against us at any time. Corporations have layoffs, churches ask pastors to leave, the economy sours and companies go under. What happens when I lose employment? Consider the words of **Matthew 6:25-26**

> 25 " Therefore I say to you, do not worry about your life, what you will eat or what you will drink; nor about your body, what you will put on. Is not life more than food and the body more than clothing?
> 26 "Look at the birds of the air, for they neither sow nor reap nor gather into barns; yet your heavenly Father feeds them. Are you not of more value than they?

Who meets our needs? We'll see this clearly when we look at the rest of Jeremiah's declaration. For now, it's important to understand that when we look to any other source than God for our strength (be that financial, emotional, or spiritual strength), we are already under the curse. Why? The flesh is corrupted and falls short of God's plan.

Every person struggles with flesh and the corruption of sin. Sin is the curse. The curse came by sin. Anything corrupted by the curse of sin is a curse to any who place their hope in it. People are imperfect. We all have the flesh and we all see the world through selfish eyes. We strive to overcome our selfish nature, but we still filter everything through our own flawed perspective.

The one who puts their hope in people is putting their hope in the flesh. Their heart departs from the Lord because they are looking to something other than the Lord for their trust. Where your eyes are looking, your life will follow. Try walking straight while looking to the side. Your direction will drift to where you are looking. When another person is your hope, your life will follow that person and when they let you down, it will shake you. Depending on the circumstances, it could shatter you. If they drift off course (which we all do from time to time), any who follow will drift with them.

A Blessed Confidence

When you are dependent upon people or circumstances, you will not see the good when it comes. Think about that statement for a moment. Why would we not see when good comes? What happens when someone irritates us? Or fails to do what we think needs to be done? When we are frustrated, what do we think about? All of our focus zeroes in on what bothers us and we cannot see anything but the source of our frustration. If you have a hundred good things in your life, and one thing frustrates you, which do you focus on? The hundred good things, or the one bad thing?

When someone we are dependent upon for our emotional health fails us, what state does that leave us in? If you love someone because they made you happy, but now that person fails to do so, what happens to your love? It becomes disappointment, then frustration, anger, and finally bitterness or even hatred.

The truth is, many people are in love with happiness, and the heart of their relationship revolves around self-love. Have you witnessed a bitter divorce? How do two lovebirds become mortal enemies? Sometimes marriages fall apart suddenly. People seem to be getting along one moment, and then at war the next. The truth is, the foundation has been eroding for some time, and when the walls begin to fall, the whole marriage collapses quickly.

A bitter spouse cannot see good. A bitter person cannot see good. They are like a shrub in the desert and cannot see good, even when it comes into their presence. The reason they cannot see good is because they can only see what disappoints. And it all begins with placing our hope into a person who has no more ability to make us happy than we do ourselves. It's unfair for me to make my happiness dependent upon my wife's abilities. This is selfish, destructive, and gives her a burden she cannot carry for long. If I can't make myself happy, how can I expect someone else to do this for me? If my spouse can't be happy in the Lord, I have no power to overcome this shortfall either.

The reality of life is if I'm looking at people for my satisfaction, it puts me into the desert. I will not be satisfied through people. Human nature cannot rise to the level of perfection needed to sustain happiness. When people fail me, if they are my hope, I will only see what's lacking and cannot see the good around me. Or the good in that person.

The picture the Bible gives is that of a dry shrub in a salted desert. This vivid illustration paints an accurate picture of a bitter heart. Nothing good can satisfy the bitter heart and it won't recognize good when it comes. But the opposite is true for the blessed heart. Let's continue beyond God's warning in **Jeremiah 17** and see the promise.

7 "Blessed *is* the man who trusts in the LORD, And whose hope is the LORD.

8 For he shall be like a tree planted by the waters, Which spreads out its roots by the river, And will not fear when heat comes; But its leaf will be green, And will not be anxious in the year of drought, Nor will cease from yielding fruit.

9 "The heart *is* deceitful above all *things,* And desperately wicked; Who can know it?

10 I, the LORD, search the heart, *I* test the mind, Even to give every man according to his ways, According to the fruit of his doings.

Is there a greater picture of true satisfaction? Years ago we had a severe drought where I live. It didn't rain for a couple of months, and the hot summer heat parched what little moisture was left in the ground. I took a walk in a national park and saw the dry trees shedding their leaves. It looked like winter. Nothing was green and nothing looked alive. It was a pitiful sight.

As I walked, I descended a hill where a stream was. The stream was still flowing with water and the trees around it were teeming with life. Not only were they unaffected by the drought, they were unaware there was a drought. This is the picture God is painting in Jeremiah.

The one whose hope is in the Lord will never be barren in their soul, nor will fear the year of drought. The word in verse 8 which says 'fear' is the Hebrew word, 'ra'ah', which means to see, perceive, or consider. Literally, this promise of God is saying we will not perceive the drought when it comes because we are planted by God's river.

The truth God is communicating is that life is full of hard times, difficulties, and things that challenge the world around us. Anyone not planted by the waters of God's providing hand will dry up. Those dependent upon circumstances and people will be frustrated, disappointed, and likely will become bitter. However, those whose hope is in the Lord will not be in the desert, will not experience the drought, and will not wither from the dry heat of life.

Do you see the incredible promise of God? Even in the most difficult circumstances, you cannot only survive, but will flourish, be fruitful, and unaffected by life's scorching heat. Your friends will fail you, but God sustains. Your spouse will disappoint you, but God fulfills. The Lord is your provider and He is your trust. If you trust in the flesh (other people or circumstances), you'll miss the good even when it comes. If your trust and hope is in the Lord, you will flourish and be fruitful, even when people fall short, disappoint you, and even when they turn against you.

Our hope becomes either a blessing or a curse. When we trust in something that is prone to failure, our expectations fail with it. But when we trust in the Lord, who never fails, our hope is always sustained, for the Lord upholds us with His hand.

The things of this life are either eternal or temporal. Anything temporal is rooted in the flesh, but the eternal is grounded in the Lord. Trusting in the flesh is to put our hope in money, careers, or any person or circumstance.

When life is viewed through the eyes of the flesh, it often isn't fair. People wrong one another and often get away with it. I recently read a book about a family who faithfully served the Lord[24]. A politically powerful man in their small town decided the pastor had to go. The persecution the family endured was almost unbelievable. Through it all, the family remained faithful to God and taught their children not to harbor bitterness, but to pray for and forgive their persecutors. Even when the persecution grew into violence, this godly family refused to retaliate, but constantly reminded the young children to forgive and trust the Lord.

I expected to see a miracle of God to intervene to stop the persecution, but the persecutor finally won his battle to drive the family out of the town. The family had given refuge to a woman fleeing her violent husband. Seeing an opportunity, the pastor's enemy helped the husband to become intoxicated, worked him up emotionally, gave him a gun, and sent him into the home with the intent to kill. The pastor and his wife were shot and she died at the scene.

When I read this I was stunned. Why didn't God stop the persecutors? The man who pulled the trigger got a long prison sentence, but the one who tormented the pastor's family for years and orchestrated the attack received only one year in prison. What a horrible injustice! Because he was politically connected, the man who rejoiced while the ambulances took away a shattered family received a mere slap on the wrist. But then something happened.

The man emerged from prison after one year a changed person. He then made it his life's ambition to do good to the remaining family members and asked their forgiveness. In prison, someone shared the gospel, and he finally understood the message, and surrendered his life to Christ.

Humanly speaking, we want God to miraculously strike down the wicked who seeks to destroy the righteous. There are times when this does happen, but not always. Often God asks His children to endure persecution and not to love their lives in this world. A godly man and woman made it their

---

[24] The Devil in Pew Number Seven

life's mission to do good to many (including to their persecutor) but ended up losing everything. Yet, during the years of persecution, they prayed for God to change the heart of the man who hated them.

Which is the greater miracle? Striking down the wicked, or changing the unchangeable? A man who paced back and forth in front of their house for years, ranting in the early morning hours and shaking his fist at the godly family who lived there, was changed by the love he saw. A love he thought he hated.

Now let's compare the temporal to the eternal. Was it fair that God allowed a faithful family to suffer so much? Was it fair for two children to lose the mother they loved and see their father destroyed by the ungodly? If we look at this situation through the scope of our 70-year life on earth, this is a horrible tragedy and a grievous injustice. What kind of a loving God would allow the innocent to be destroyed by the wicked? In the 70-year perspective, there is no way this is a fair result. However, if we look beyond the temporary and to the eternal, everything changes.

What happens to the mother whose life was stolen? When we stand before God, what happens to the father who served God on earth at the cost of everything we as people hold dear? Will he ache at the loss of what he missed on earth? Quite the opposite! To give up what is destined to pass away in order to gain what is eternal is not a sacrifice, but an investment in eternity. Not one person will grieve in heaven for what he or she sacrificed on earth. On the other hand, many people will grieve over what they forfeited in heaven for a few days on earth. Consider **Joel 2:25-26**

25 "So I will restore to you the years that the swarming locust has eaten, The crawling locust, The consuming locust, And the chewing locust, My great army which I sent among you.
26 You shall eat in plenty and be satisfied, And praise the name of the LORD your God, Who has

dealt wondrously with you; And My people shall never be put to shame.

This is a promise to Israel, but the principle applies to us all. When God's promise becomes reality, will we mourn over what was consumed by the locusts of the earth? No. We will rejoice over God's restoration, and we'll see what the New Testament states, "No eye has seen nor ear heard what God has in store for those who love Him." Or as the Apostle Paul stated, "The sufferings of this present time are not worthy to be compared with the glory that will be revealed in us."

What lies ahead is not worthy to even be compared to this life; therefore, what we lose is nothing. It's not even worth considering. But we have to have an eternal perspective to see this truth. We can't see this unless our lives are looking through the lens of eternity instead of through the eyes of this temporary life.

What problems are you enduring? What wrongs have been done to you? What sacrifices are you forced to endure – or are being called to make?

We get angry and bitter at people and God, and this is because we are looking at life through the trust we have in the flesh. We can't see the good of God's will because we focus on the temporal good our flesh demands. I say good in the fleshly sense, but in truth, God is the only provider of good. We think pleasure is good, wealth is good, relationships are good, etc. While these things have their place, they are a poor substitute for the good of eternity.

When we have to endure hardships, if our trust is in the flesh (the things which make us happy in this life) we cannot see when true good comes. Jesus said, "He who loves his life will lose it, but he who hates his life in this world will keep it for eternal life." To hate our life in this world doesn't mean we despise life or ourselves. It means we don't consider our life in this world worthy to be compared to what lies ahead. It's to be willing to endure difficulties, persecutions, problems, and loss in light of God's perfect will and the kingdom we will inherit.

It's the Lord who promised that all things work for the good of those who love God and are called according to His purposes.

Do I truly believe this? If so, I'll put my trust in God's purposes and the good behind it rather than in people, things, and circumstances. This promise is to those who are walking according to God's purposes; therefore, we must seek to know God and look for His will over our own. This is a lifelong process and is something we have to daily seek.

Today's victory won't be tomorrow's triumph. Each day is a new willful choice to surrender and walk in God's purposes. Each situation we face is a choice to seek God's will, or focus on the desires and preservation of our flesh.

To seek our own pleasure makes happiness and joy dependent upon what we can gain. We would then be required to control our circumstances in order to find joy. Since it's impossible to control every circumstance, joy will always be just out of reach.

When we seek God's will, He becomes our reward and our satisfaction. Only then do we have the promise, "You prepared a table before me in the presence of my enemies," and, "You give me to drink from the river of Your pleasures." The Bible says when God blesses, He adds no sorrow with it.[25] God's pleasure never includes regret or consequences. However, the true promise is what lies at the end of this journey.

The blessed confidence is in those who say, "Not my will, but Yours." Anything outside of God's will leads us to the parched places in the wilderness. Do not allow people to be your source for happiness. Enjoy relationships through God, not outside of Him. Then love others without conditions. Let's conclude this chapter with **Proverbs 11:24**

---

[25] Proverbs 10:22

There is *one* who scatters, yet increases more; And there is *one* who withholds more than is right, But it *leads* to poverty.

How true this proverb is in relationships. The person who seeks love often lacks it. Emotionally needy people are takers, yet they are never fulfilled. They often fall into emotional poverty. The person who takes the love God has poured out into their hearts (see Romans 5:5) and scatters it into the lives of those around them, will increase with more than they have given.

Love is the thing which grows more abundantly as it is given away. But it becomes scarce as we take it from others. Love isn't a treasure protected within the heart, but a fountain which must flow outward. Love is something given to us by God's grace. Just as He expresses love toward us while we are at odds with Him[26], we also must give His love to others – both to those who deserve it and those who do not. Hoarded love stagnates into self-centeredness, but love given away returns in abundance.

In this assurance from God we find our blessed confidence.

---

[26] Romans 5:8-10

A Blessed Confidence

# Life Applications

- Memorize 1 Corinthians 13:4-7
- Evaluate how you define love against the passage above.
- Consider the ways you have withheld love in your relationships. What happens when love is conditional?
- Identify relationships that are lacking in love as God has defined it. Plan ways to show love without requiring anything in return.
- Pray for the power to give with no other motivation than to express faith in God's commands and promises.
- Review Life Applications from previous chapters.

# Cultivating a Thankful Heart

**Isaiah 26:3**

You will keep *him* in perfect peace, *Whose* mind *is* stayed *on You,* Because he trusts in You.

The above passage is at the heart of thanksgiving. The Bible instructs us to do all things without complaining and disputing.[27] The grumbler does not see good in what he or she is doing. A complainer has a hot head and a cold heart.

When we are in this state, we don't recognize the goodness of God's hand. When we find ourselves in a difficult, uncomfortable, or even a painful situation, we say, "God why? Why did you let this happen? Why did you do this? Why don't you fix it?" Or the most common complaint, "Why do I always have to...."

If you've read the story of the Exodus, you know how God delivered the Jewish people from the oppression of Pharaoh. God took them from slavery, delivered them from the pursuing army, and sent them through the desert as they journeyed toward the promise of their inheritance. It was an inheritance guaranteed by God's own covenant with their forefather, Abraham.

When the people became thirsty, God gave them water. When they were hungry, God sent manna from heaven. The Lord met every need, yet the people couldn't see God's hand in their lives. They could only see the sand of the desert. They complained about the food, the journey, the leadership, and the things they left behind. The very people who cried out to God for deliverance from the hard bondage of slavery began to say, "Oh that we were back in Egypt." Some even formed a party and prepared to return back to the land of bondage.

Their unthankful hearts not only blinded them to God's grace, but it also caused them to forget what they had

---

[27] Philippians 2:14

escaped from. What originally had been intended as a few weeks of journeying toward an inheritance, suddenly appeared as less desirable than a lifetime of bondage.

We look back at the foolishness of these people and are amazed they could be so blind. Yet this is the picture of the Christian life. We were under the bondage of sin, but God delivered us, defeated Satan, and set us on a journey through the desert. We often forget, this Christian life *is* a journey through the desert of this world. The Bible says, "Blessed is the one whose strength is in you, whose heart is on a pilgrimage."[28]

Is your heart on a pilgrimage? Are you living life as though you are journeying toward something better? Or do you look at this life as the prize? This directly affects how we respond to the circumstances of life.

There are times when the journey seems long and tiring. Sometimes we are uncomfortable, miserable, and want something different. It is during those times when we have to stop and think about not only where we are, but consider where we are going. This is why the Bible says to adopt the attitude of Christ. For the joy set before Jesus, He endured the cross even though He despised its shame.[29] The shame didn't disappear, nor did Jesus escape the thing He despised. He endured it, not because he changed His circumstances, but because He looked beyond that to the goal – our reconciliation and redemption.

We are also in the same position each time we are in the midst of circumstances we don't like. Though it may not be as severe as the cross, we become weary when we forget where we are going. When we forget we are on a pilgrimage – a journey through a land that isn't our destination – we can easily become discouraged. Don't try to make the desert your home. Life can be hard, but there are times of refreshing. However, this refreshment is to prepare us for

---

[28] Psalm 84:5

[29] Hebrews 12:2

the next leg of the journey. Let's look at the wonderful thoughts of King David's journey in **Psalm 23:1-6**

¹ The LORD *is* my shepherd; I shall not want.

² He makes me to lie down in green pastures; He leads me beside the still waters.

³ He restores my soul; He leads me in the paths of righteousness For His name's sake.

⁴ Yea, though I walk through the valley of the shadow of death, I will fear no evil; For You *are* with me; Your rod and Your staff, they comfort me.

⁵ You prepare a table before me in the presence of my enemies; You anoint my head with oil; My cup runs over.

⁶ Surely goodness and mercy shall follow me All the days of my life; And I will dwell in the house of the LORD Forever.

Take a moment to reflect on this passage. First, we are being led somewhere. Like Israel in the desert, God is leading us from a life of being bound by sin and worthless passions to the promised home He has prepared for us. Take to heart the words of Jesus, "I go to prepare a place for you and will come again to receive you." That is our destination. We live in a fallen world and even if we could control every aspect of our lives, the world around us would still be fallen, and it would fall short of what God has prepared for us.

Take note of verses two and three in Psalms above. They are the preparation for verse four. God restores our soul and gives us good things and times of renewal, but this isn't our reward. It is the rest for the next leg of the journey.

When we forget this, we begin murmuring when our Shepherd leads us into the valley. That valley can be ugly. It can be fearful. It can cast the shadow of death all around us. Yet, we must pass through the valley because it's between us and our destination.

Even in the horrible valley, there is still peace and comfort – if we have eyes to see it. We can rest in the comfort that God is with us and protects us. As David expressed, though he walks in the valley, he doesn't fear – for God protects with His rod and staff. The rod is a weapon, the staff is correction. When a sheep drifts off course, the staff had a hooked end and the shepherd would reach out and stop the sheep from walking into danger. The rod is the weapon the shepherd used against predators who threatened the sheep.

What should be a great encouragement is that even in the valley, with enemies all around, God prepares a table before us where we can dine and have fellowship with Him. This isn't the time of refreshing we'll experience when we arrive to the next green pasture. This is the strength and encouragement of God's fellowship in the midst of turmoil.

The enemies may be around us, but we still experience fellowship with our God. The enemy could be people, hazards, hardships, or our own internal struggles. Yet as we allow God to lead us through this valley, we are renewed in the midst of hardship. We may still be in our difficulties, but not without the strength and fellowship of our God. There is a peace of God which can be found in the midst of any valley. But we must have eyes of faith in order to see it.

## Stay Focused on Joy

Now let's go back to the historical illustration of our Christian journey – Israel's journey through the desert. They truly only had two options, return to bondage, or journey through the desert. Nothing good can come from returning to Egypt, just as nothing good can come from abandoning our pilgrimage of faith and returning to living for the world.

Why were so many tempted to abandon God's leading? They lost sight of where they were going and began to focus on where they were and what they wanted now.

There is a firm truth in this historical biblical illustration. God gave us the historical account of Israel for a reason – it is our example.[30] They missed the promise because they could only see what they had lost and what they were going through. Quickly they forgot the promise of where they were journeying to and they forgot the bondage of where they had come from.

We do the same thing with sin. When we forget the harm it caused in our lives, we then look at it as if it were a benefit. We crave it because we forget how it desires to rule over us. Temptation is a call to submit back into the slavery of the flesh. This is what Israel faced. They forgot the hardship they left and only looked at the things they craved. They forgot the promise of where they were going, so they could only see the hardship of the journey. They forgot to be thankful for God's daily provision, and the joy of what He was leading them toward.

Hardship seems pointless if there is no joy before us. Joy causes us to look beyond our circumstances (as Christ did) and to the reward on the other side. I know I'm repeating this illustration, but it's important for us to fully grasp the purpose of joy. Jesus endured the cross, not because He wanted the cross. He despised it. Three times He begged for another way,[31] yet He endured for the joy set before Him.

Hebrews 12:3 reminds us to look at this very example so we do not become weary in our souls. If you forget the joy, you will grow weary in the journey. But if you look at the joy set before you, endurance will come from the Lord. Don't forget the promise we looked at earlier, "The joy of the Lord is my strength."[32]

Joy is not like happiness. Happiness is dependent on circumstances. If I get a new job or pay raise, I'm happy. A house or car makes me happy for a moment. Anytime I get what I want, I'm happy for a short time. But what happens

---

[30] 1 Corinthians 10:6, 11; Hebrews 4:11

[31] Matthew 26:39

[32] Nehemiah 8:10

when my marriage has trials, my job becomes stressful, or my car breaks down? Any time circumstances take a turn for the worse, I'm no longer happy.

Circumstances can't rob me of joy – unless I put my hope in something other than Christ. Joy is not looking at what I have, but at the promises of the Lord. Some of those promises will be revealed in this lifetime, but most will not. The promise of God is eternal. Our promise is like the Promised Land God gave to the Jews. Many didn't believe and never found the promise, but God raised a people who would enter. They journeyed long and hard to reach the promise. It was their rest. We too are journeying to a promise. Our promise is not this fallen world. Many promises do apply to this life, but 'the promise' applies to the day when we finish this journey and our faith becomes sight.

I've said all of this to lay the foundation of thanksgiving. Thanksgiving is the health of the Christian soul. Unless we understand the pilgrimage of our lives, we won't have a solid foundation in which to understand thankfulness. When thankfulness is dependent upon positive circumstances, our hearts will fall short of this command.

Yes, thanksgiving is a command, and understandably so. If God provides the miracle of manna in the desert, is it too much to expect a heart of gratitude from a people who would have otherwise starved?

When did the people begin to despise God's provisioning of manna? They grew tired of eating it because they looked back to where they had come from and said, "They are eating better than we are." They should have looked forward and said, "When we get to the promise, we'll have a land flowing with milk and honey." One attitude looks at what we don't have. The other attitude looks at what God promises we will have. Neither attitude changes the circumstances, but one acknowledges God's goodness and provision while the other despises what God is doing.

Thanksgiving is rooted in faith – believing the promises of God. This attitude of thanksgiving changes the way each of us approach life and our relationship with God.

## Be Thankful – all things work for good!

**Romans 8:27-28**

27 Now He who searches the hearts knows what the mind of the Spirit *is,* because He makes intercession for the saints according to *the will of* God.
28 And we know that all things work together for good to those who love God, to those who are the called according to *His* purpose.

What does it mean that all things work together for our good? The first thing we must understand is how good should be defined. In our human nature, we tend to measure goodness based on how we feel or whether we are getting what we want. We define 'good' based on life in this world, but God defines 'good' based on eternity.

When it comes to difficult circumstances, if it doesn't make me feel good, I don't think of it as good. If I lose my job, I'll come home and say, "I have bad news." From the temporary perspective, hardship always looks bad. Yet there are bad things in my life where I look back and realize it was indeed good. I can look back and see how circumstances forced me to go where I didn't want to go, but I now see the goodness of God in those circumstances. And how what I thought was a bad problem was actually a door for God to bless me in ways I would never have experienced.

This is true for our life in this world, but how much more true is this in our life to come. God will sacrifice your temporal comfort for your eternal good. We may look at painful situations as tragedies, but that's because we are measuring things against our perceived needs and desires. These desires are felt through a body of flesh that can only understand a temporary world and short-term comfort.

Shortsighted human nature looks at our situation and compares it to what we believe will make us happy. A thankful heart looks at the promise in the scripture above and compares it to our circumstances, then understands that because God is working all things to our good, the end result will always be good. The truth is all good things have their roots in the heart of God; therefore, to find good we have to be in the will of God. And we have to trust Him enough to abide in Him and obey, regardless of how we feel.

When I walk in my own ways, I can never have confidence that hardship is for my good. Without discovering the heart of God and His love toward me, I also cannot understand what is truly good.

Good is measured against God and His eternal purposes, not against my feelings or comfort. Many times God's good will indeed make me happy, but sometimes it does not. That's because what I think is good isn't always good. The path I think is right doesn't always lead to what is right. I can only see the short term view of what appears good, but the Lord sees all things, for He sees the end from the beginning, and is able to turn even the most difficult circumstance into a blessing. The Lord will also take us through difficulties in order to obtain the greater blessing.

God will test you. God will allow things into your life that will challenge your faith and attempt to rob you of joy and thanksgiving. He does so only after giving us the power to endure and the faith to believe. Faith is hoping for what is not yet seen.[33] The one who begins to grumble will not see the fullness of God's blessing. They will often miss the promise that can only be received by faith. Let's go back to our illustration of the desert for an example.

After enduring many hardships, God took the children of Israel to the edge of the promise. God did not require faith until the time came to inherit the Promised Land. The Lord delivered a faithless people from the land of bondage. He

---

[33] Romans 8:24-26

defeated the army which pursued them after they left. He fed them with manna and provided water from a rock. He covered them from the heat by a cloud and met their every need. All the while, God told them He was taking them to the land of promise. Then one day they arrived. Standing on the bank of a river, the people camped while God instructed twelve men to go and spy out the land. It was a test of their faith.

Twelve spies explored the land and returned with their report. Their word was, "Everything is just as God described it. The land is truly flowing with milk and honey as God promised. But – there are giants in the land and we cannot stand against them." As the people heard the report of the dangers which threatened them, they wept in disappointment, and then revolted. They refused to cross the river because of the hardships and trials that looked threatening.

What did God do? He sent them back into the desert. They couldn't inherit the promise because they trusted the circumstances over the Lord. Is this not what we do? How many seemingly faithful Christians turned back because the road was too hard? Indeed it is too hard. It's supposed to be. God is calling us to go where we cannot go and do what we cannot do by our own strength. Facing the giants on our own leads to certain defeat, for they are greater than we are. But they are not greater than the Shepherd who leads us.

He leads us into the valley to prove our faith. Those who emerge on the other side do so because they have learned to trust God in the storms of life. Those who don't, turn back and never discover what God had for them. But all good is found within God's purposes, not our own.

Thankfulness is not looking at circumstances and problems, but looking to God to lead us through and believing His promise that good awaits beyond our hardships. Consider **Psalm 139:14-18**

14 I will praise You, for I am fearfully *and*
wonderfully made; Marvelous are Your works, And

Cultivating a Thankful Heart

*that* my soul knows very well.

15 My frame was not hidden from You, When I was made in secret, *And* skillfully wrought in the lowest parts of the earth.

16 Your eyes saw my substance, being yet unformed. And in Your book they all were written, The days fashioned for me, When *as yet there were* none of them.

17 How precious also are Your thoughts to me, O God! How great is the sum of them!

18 *If* I should count them, they would be more in number than the sand;

Do you realize that God formed you as you are? And fashioned the days of your life before you were born? When Moses struggled to trust God because of his speech impediment, God said, "Who made man's mouth? Or who makes the mute, the deaf, the seeing, or the blind? Have not I, the LORD?"

You mean God is behind my physical struggles? According to God's own words, yes. Why is someone born blind, unattractive, beautiful, imperfect, weak, or strong? This isn't for us to fully know, but one thing we do know, God has it as part of His plan. Just as God used Moses as a leader of Israel, who spoke before kings in spite of his speech problems, God also uses us to accomplish His purposes in spite of our shortcomings. If anything, our shortcomings become a blessing because we learn what it means to depend on God and not our own abilities.

Does this mean life should be easy? Certainly not. Overcoming is difficult. If it were not so challenging, Jesus would not have said the greatest promises are "To him who overcomes." Him refers to both men and women, for it is in reference to mankind in the general sense. Overcoming is a challenge, and it isn't something we have fully accomplished until we are standing firm on the rock of Christ and walking in God's will.

The Apostle Paul had a physical problem which deeply troubled him. It was something related to his appearance because he praised the church of Galatia for not rejecting him because of it. After three times of begging God for healing, the Lord showed this was of God and served to make Paul weak so he could experience God's strength.

Each weakness or limitation we have only serves to reveal God's power in us – for as Paul said, "Most gladly I will rather boast in my infirmities, that the power of Christ may rest upon me. When I am weak, then I am strong."[34]

We depend upon ourselves when we feel confident and strong, but when we are in need, we depend upon God. That is when we discover true strength – when we get out of the way and allow God to reveal Himself through us.

When we acknowledge our weakness before God, His strength becomes our foundation. This same truth applies to any circumstance in our lives that we cannot handle. Rather than crumbling under the weight of our problems or grumbling against God for our circumstances, we must learn to cast our cares upon the Lord. Learn to be strong in Him, acknowledge our weaknesses, and take confidence in His strength.

# Rejoice Always

**1 Peter 1:6-9**

> 6 In this you greatly rejoice, though now for a little while, if need be, you have been grieved by various trials,
>
> 7 that the genuineness of your faith, *being* much more precious than gold that perishes, though it is tested by fire, may be found to praise, honor, and glory at the revelation of Jesus Christ,
>
> 8 whom having not seen you love. Though now you do not see *Him,* yet believing, you rejoice with joy

---

[34] 2 Corinthians 12:8-10

inexpressible and full of glory,
⁹ receiving the end of your faith -- the salvation of
*your* souls.

Rejoicing and having a heart of thanksgiving does not mean we deny that problems exist. Though we may be grieved by various trials, the heart founded upon a genuine faith has the ability to rejoice in God through these trials. Once again, the rejoicing is possible by looking beyond our struggles and to the coming promise that will one day be revealed.

Giving thanks in all things doesn't mean I have to thank God for the pain I may have to endure; it's to thank God for what lies beyond the pain and heartache. It's the realization that trials are for the perfecting of the saints. Through these hardships, I know I will experience something greater than what I lost. Let's look ahead to the Apostle Peter's explanation in **1 Peter 4:12-13**

¹² Beloved, do not think it strange concerning the
fiery trial which is to try you, as though some
strange thing happened to you;
¹³ but rejoice to the extent that you partake of
Christ's sufferings, that when His glory is revealed,
you may also be glad with exceeding joy.

What are we being called to rejoice in? The trial? No. We are rejoicing that we are partakers of Christ's sufferings *so* we also may be partakers of His glory. Throughout the scriptures, we are promised if we are faithful, we'll inherit the Kingdom of God, reign with Christ, and receive every promise in scripture. Add to that, God hasn't yet revealed all that awaits us. But just as was the case with those wandering through the desert, if we turn from God during the trials, we miss the promise.

A murmuring spirit doesn't acknowledge God is working for our good. What a loss it will be if we endure life with bitterness and never profit from what we have to endure. God's goal is not to merely try us for the sake of trials, but to bring about good and lead us to the glory yet to be revealed. Let's add one more passage to help explain one of the purposes of trials. Look at **Hebrews 12:27-28**

27 Now this, "Yet once more," indicates the removal of those things that are being shaken, as of things that are made, that the things which cannot be shaken may remain.

28 Therefore, since we are receiving a kingdom which cannot be shaken, let us have grace, by which we may serve God acceptably with reverence and godly fear.

Many things are shaken for the purpose of proving what is of God and what is not – such as the earth, the church, and us as individuals. Our spiritual lives are founded upon the immovable rock of Christ. However, our lives in the flesh are not. When circumstances shake our lives, anything that is not of God is shaken. Anything secure in the Spirit remains unshakeable. Sometimes trials prove us – whether we are truly in the Spirit. Other times it is to shake loose the things of the flesh – for the flesh can't remain unshaken when tried.

Often times we think we are spiritual, but we are still carrying the burden of the flesh in many areas. Trials shake these things free. The person who is clinging to the flesh will fight against God because they are unwilling to allow the Lord to shake loose the fleshly things of their heart.

Other times we may sorrow, but still trust Him as He prunes our lives. As we grow in the faith, we'll learn what Peter is teaching – to rejoice in the trials knowing God is purifying our souls.

When an unexpected tragedy strikes, does it catch God off guard? No. He has already made a way through the trial and has His goodness prepared to be received on the other side. At times God has prepared a miraculous deliverance, and other times we must endure trials. To us who are called and following God's purposes, all things work for our good.

If a circumstance threatens us and is not something God is using for our good, He will deliver us from it. If He does not deliver, it is something which will produce good in our lives – either now, or for our eternal good. It's God's good pleasure to give you His kingdom.[35] Sometimes part of our old life has to be removed so we can receive the Kingdom and new life.

Now let us consider **Colossians 3:15**

[15] And let the peace of God rule in your hearts, to which also you were called in one body; and be thankful.

The one body referred to in this passage is the collection of all believers. We are one body, the people of God. Though we have many churches and denominations, anyone who belongs to Christ is part of the body of Christ, the universal church. Church unity begins the same way a thankful heart begins – by letting the peace of God rule in our hearts. Peace rules when there is nothing else on the throne but Christ. Thankfulness is once again at the center of the right attitude and a heart of peace.

A thankful heart is a trusting heart. Trust produces thanksgiving. It does so because our faith opens our eyes to see beyond the circumstances to the goodness God is working. Even if we don't see how our individual hardship is going to be resolved, we still can look ahead to the goodness of God, knowing He is leading us to every promise.

One truth must always be at the forefront. God seeks my good. Because this is true, my current situation is part of God's plan to deliver His goodness into my life. I may only see the valley, but I can look back and see the good He has already done, look ahead to the promises of what He will do, and then be assured that beyond the valley is a goodness He

---

[35] Luke 12:32

will bring. I don't have to see it to hope for it. I merely have to believe His word.

This is why God instructs me to come before Him with prayers and supplications with thanksgiving. I can be thankful, even when I don't see beyond my next step. Is it hard to be thankful when things seem difficult? You bet it is.

Anyone can have faith when the road is smooth. Everyone is thankful when getting what they want. But faith is proven when the road is difficult and the only good I see is the promise of the word. Then I know it lies ahead and I can be thankful even as I present my prayers for God's strength during my hardship. While I pour out my grief before Him, I can also be thankful and rejoice in what He is leading me toward. **1 Thessalonians 5:16-18** explains:

16 Rejoice always,

17 pray without ceasing,

18 in everything give thanks; for this is the will of God in Christ Jesus for you.

If you can't give thanks in everything, it is not possible to fully experience the will of God in your life.

If you and I can live by this passage, we will do well. It is through these things God gives us the promise that His peace will guard our hearts and minds through Christ. How would it change our lives if we consistently practiced the above passage – even when we don't feel like it? Even when we don't understand?

Learn to cultivate a thankful heart and you will accomplish God's will and experience the fullness of joy. It's a promise. Rejoice in that promise!

# Life Applications

- Do you find yourself grumbling? Let this remind you to take your eyes off the circumstance and look ahead to the promises of God.
- Memorize Hebrews 12:1-3
- Think about something God has promised that gives you hope. When something troubles your heart, practice dealing with the problem while keeping your focus on what gives you hope and joy.
- Memorize Romans 8:27-28
- Take time out to thank God for the good you see.
- Meditate on your life. Think of the good things which show God's hand. Think about the times when problems ended up leading you to a blessing. Consider these things when you see problems today.
- Let God shake loose the things He is removing.
- Set ten minutes aside each day to thank God for all things. Name the good and the things He is using for a future good.
- Learn to rejoice in the Lord always.
    - When troubled, rejoice in the promises and His refining process.
    - When happy, rejoice in the time of refreshing.
- Take time to review previous Life Applications.

# Planting and Cultivating

We've touched on this topic briefly, but in this chapter we'll dig deeper into how our daily decisions affect life as a whole. Today is the day to prepare for tomorrow's harvest. Let's learn how to grow into maturity by sowing the seeds of joy with intent and purpose.

If a farmer plants corn, he can expect to reap corn. If he plants wheat, he'll reap wheat. Obvious, right? What if he planted weeds, thorns, and briars? Could he expect to reap wheat, corn, or anything of value? Of course not. Yet this is exactly what we do in our daily lives. We invest our lives in valueless endeavors, but then we expect to be fruitful. If I invest my time and energy in negativism, can I expect a return of peace, joy, or happiness? Can I expect a cheerful outlook when I'm cultivating negative emotions in my heart and mind?

The next time you wonder, "Why am I so down?" stop and examine your investments. Consider the words of **Galatians 6:7-9**

7 Do not be deceived, God is not mocked; for whatever a man sows, that he will also reap.

8 For he who sows to his flesh will of the flesh reap corruption, but he who sows to the Spirit will of the Spirit reap everlasting life.

9 And let us not grow weary while doing good, for in due season we shall reap if we do not lose heart.

Remember our earlier discussions about the flesh? The flesh cannot produce anything but the things of the flesh. To reap the things we value as Christians, we must sow in the Spirit. Only then can peace, love, and joy come to maturity in our lives.

Let's look deeper into this and see how to apply it to everyday life. We'll look at sowing in the Spirit in a moment, but first let's look at the contrast between sowing for either corruption or good. Well doing begins in the heart. We are commanded to love others and to do good from a pure heart. It's not possible to serve God and do good works without first dealing with your own heart.

Can you produce good from a heart that is destined to reap corruption? Certainly not. We establish good works from a heart that has already been established in the grace of the Lord. All good comes from God. We receive from God, grow in grace, and then God's goodness comes out in our lives.

The first warning in the above passage is, God is not mocked. The word mocked comes from the Greek word, 'mukterizo', which means: to thumb the nose.

Few of us would think of ourselves as thumbing our noses at God, but there is a significant truth for us to consider. When David sinned, God said, "You have despised Me." When the people refused to live in obedience, God said, "You have no right to claim my covenant seeing you hate instructions and cast my words behind you."[36]

To know the truth and to cast it behind us is to mock God. This is true even if the truth we reject seems insignificant to us. It's the little things that lay the foundation for the bigger things of life.

This chapter might come across as a little harsh, but hang with me here. This isn't intended to be judgmental. It's the straight truth. And it's what I've had to learn the hard way (and am still learning). Sometimes we need a good jolt every now and then. It's far too easy to get into a funk and stay there, but applying these truths forces us into action.

The harsh reality is when we need to apply God's principles the most, we want to do it the least. Yet to neglect these things puts us on a path of grief. We need to be reminded by someone who cares enough to stand in our way and tell us we are making foolish decisions. And that is what some of these hard scriptures are doing. They may sound harsh, but it is the voice of God's love.

---

[36] Psalm 50

Every time I choose to neglect the word, I am making a foolish choice. The choice is not only affecting my momentary state, but I'm setting in motion a harvest in my life which will either benefit me, or further corrupt my heart.

Before I go on, let me qualify my above statement. The corruption we experience is our life in the flesh. While it's hard not to doubt our salvation when we drift far from God, the truth is that the consequences of our choices aren't necessarily speaking of eternal life. There are consequences and rewards. We'll be held accountable for the life we live in this world, but this doesn't mean the Christian will lose eternal life. But it does mean we will regret our bad choices.

If we care nothing about spiritual things, the Bible calls us to examine ourselves to see if we are truly in the faith. This chapter isn't intended to create doubt, but to show us how to find confidence. The consequences of disregarding God's word are often in this life as well as forfeiting many promises in the life to come.

For example, the Corinthian church had a man living in a very immoral lifestyle. Though later he was restored, while he was actively living in corruption, the following instruction was given to the church, "Deliver such a one to Satan for the destruction of the flesh, that his spirit may be saved in the day of the Lord Jesus."[37]

His life was put into turmoil for the purpose of facing consequences now, rather than facing Christ for the consequences later. The corruption of his flesh became the consequences for his foolish actions, but it served to turn his heart to the Lord for the purpose of reconciliation – not judgment. Though he could have stiffened his neck and forced judgment, he recognized the error of his ways, repented, and was restored.[38]

---

[37] 1 Corinthians 5:5

[38] 2 Corinthians 2

Regardless of how shallow or deep we sin, the same principle applies to us. God will allow us to reap the consequences of our choices now so we have the opportunity to turn away from our own ways and toward Him. Sadly, most people never recognize the cause of their grief. They continue to invest their lives in negative behavior and wonder why they are reaping emotional damage, broken relationships, and other consequences.

I witnessed someone I care about go through this very situation. Little things bothered them. While all of us are bothered by little annoyances, this person took each annoyance into their heart and cultivated it like a cherished seed. They watered it with anger, fertilized it with bitterness, and nurture it with frustration. They could let nothing go, but everything they disliked became an offense and viewed as a threat. Their entire life was spent brooding and lashing out in anger. Before long, their problems were deep rooted and stood as a mountain of emotional turmoil in their life.

I've had many conversations with them and I get frustrated watching them. It bothers me to see them ignoring every biblical principle, and instead choosing to embrace the things that make them miserable. Life is unhappy, and until there is a change of attitude, life will always be unhappy. In fact, unless there is a change of behavior, it will get worse from here.

The truth is, each time they invest their lives into negative emotions, they are also teaching their minds to develop negative habits. The mind is like a muscle. What you invest in will become its strength. An athlete invests their time and energy into the sport they love. The result is mental reflexes and a sharpened ability which helps them excel in that sport. Some people love math (though I don't know how this is possible). As they exercise their mind, math becomes easier and they excel deeper into this skill. The same is true for any form of academic skill, physical talent, or way of thinking. This means it's also true for how we think in our daily lives.

If we develop a good attitude, we are building thought patterns which change our outlook to positive behaviors. If we develop a bad attitude, we are also teaching our minds to think in negative ways. When any situation arises where we need to engage our minds, what thought pattern do you think the mind will follow? It will be the way we have developed our ways of thinking. Everyone will have negative situations that challenge them, but those who have developed strong positive attitudes can better overcome negative emotions than those who have invested their lives into negative attitudes.

Each person will reap what they have sown into their life.

You and I have the power to derail negative emotions if we so choose, but the truth is, if I do not control my emotions on little things, I will not have the mental strength to control them on the big things. What I have invested my life in is what will come out in my character.

I had a coworker some years ago who was struggling with his emotions, and he explained his problem better than anyone I've met. He just didn't know how to handle stress. He explained his problem this way. "When you squeeze an orange, what comes out? Orange juice. When pressure hits, what is inside is what is going to come out."

He understood his own problem. When you press an orange, what is inside is what comes out. Painting an orange a different color won't change what's inside. In the same way, putting on a happy mask doesn't change your emotional make up. Most of us can put up a front to others, but when stress arises, what is inside will be what comes out in your life. Therefore, you need to begin changing what is inside. And how do we do this? The secret is found in a passage we looked at previously - **Philippians 4:4-8**

4 Rejoice in the Lord always. Again I will say, rejoice!

⁵ Let your gentleness be known to all men. The Lord *is* at hand.

⁶ Be anxious for nothing, but in everything by prayer and supplication, with thanksgiving, let your requests be made known to God;

⁷ and the peace of God, which surpasses all understanding, will guard your hearts and minds through Christ Jesus.

⁸ Finally, brethren, whatever things are true, whatever things *are* noble, whatever things *are* just, whatever things *are* pure, whatever things *are* lovely, whatever things *are* of good report, if *there is* any virtue and if *there is* anything praiseworthy -- meditate on these things.

Is this part of your daily life? When your mind is idle, do you meditate on these things? Or do you think upon the things that offend you? We all wrestle with this, though some have a more difficult time than others. For much of my life I allowed my idle mind to brood on the things that bothered me. It only built anger inside and set a pattern of thought in motion which affected many areas of my life. I can remember throwing many pity parties. Rarely did a day go by that I didn't meditate upon my frustrations.

One day the veil was pulled back and the Lord opened my eyes. I was wallowing in my usual state of feeling sorry for myself and then my thoughts shifted. I realized when I moped, no one came to console me. In fact, my attitude pushed people away. No one wants to hang around a sulky person. As I stepped back and looked at myself, I realized that no one cares if I'm feeling sorry for myself. I should have figured this out long ago, for I don't rush to join someone else's pity party either.

That was the day I began changing my way of thinking. But it isn't something that comes easy. In fact, just the other day, I was riding in the car and in a pleasant mood, but my mind slipped back into the old way of thinking. I thought of an event that happened over twenty five years ago. It was something from my military days and without realizing it, I allowed my mind to run free for a few minutes.

I didn't realize what I was doing until my anger started rising. It was a rather unpleasant situation, but certainly not worth revisiting after two and a half decades. Sometimes these memories serve to remind us of our need to forgive a wrong done. It may be that we need to pray for the person who wronged us. Once I realized my mind was brooding, I turned my focus away from it and found relief from these negative feelings. Looking at this I realize how true the scriptures' teachings are, and what a great benefit they have in our lives.

There was a time when I couldn't turn it off. I even enjoyed brooding over my problems and the wrongs done. Even thoughts of vengeance seemed pleasant. Yet, how easy it now is to put this thought away shows the value of God's ways. Once we establish ourselves in the word, it becomes easier to turn our hearts to what is good.

Looking back, I remember my parents asking why I was always down. I also remember a class mate stopping me and saying, "Why is it that you always have a frown on your face? Are you ever not sad or mad?" Another church friend in my youth group once said to me, "You are always talking bad about people. Don't you ever have anything good to say?"

I never forgot his question, for it cut me deeply. I didn't like having this type of reputation and it made me aware of my behavior. This is why the Bible says, "Faithful are the wounds of a friend." This person wounded me, but not by attacking me as a person. He pointed out my negative behavior. It wounded me in a way that revealed my need to change. I doubt those around me would say this about me today.

At the root of the problem was the focus on negative things. As long as my focus was on the bad, it came out in both my attitude and in my conversations.

The scriptures give a clear path to follow so we can reprogram our way of thinking. The ultimate problem is this battle between our flesh and the Spirit. Those who are Christ's have crucified the flesh with its passions and desires.[39] We discussed this several chapters back, but this is where it directly applies to our lives.

Your flesh will war against your mind and seek to draw you back into captivity. It's the call of two voices. In your flesh, you are called to submit back into bondage, but the Spirit of God that dwells within you[40] calls with the voice of wisdom. One call is to feed the passions of the flesh – including negative emotions, but God's call is to 'dwell on these things' as mentioned above and walk in the Spirit. One seeks to dominate your life; the other is to lead you into the joy of the Lord.

When you are feeling overwhelmed by temptation (and yes, brooding is a temptation), it's time to stop and remember the promise of God. "My old nature was crucified with Him, that the body of sin might be done away with, that I should no longer be a slave of sin."[41]

If I try to resist the emotions that enslave me, I find I'm powerless to overcome. The reason is because 'I' am trying to overcome through my own strength. Yet, when I look to Christ with eyes of faith and claim the promise, it is not 'I' who am fighting my flesh, but the Spirit of God, who has transformed me into this new life by faith, who also renews my mind by faith. I step out of the old nature which once enslaved me and into the spirit, by faith. It is God who delivered me, and I no longer have to submit myself to the bondage of my old passions.

I must want freedom before I will leave bondage.

When negative emotions seek to take over my mind, I remind myself and my flesh that the body of death has been

---

[39] Galatians 5:24

[40] 1 Corinthians 3:16

[41] Romans 6:6

done away with. It no longer has power over me. I do have the right to submit myself back into its power, but it does not have the power to overcome me, because my strength is the Lord and not my own abilities.

You and I can respond to negative situations without falling back into negative behaviors. It's not easy to keep the flesh from reacting with negative attitudes. In fact, it's impossible when I'm looking to myself. When I feel myself slipping, it's a reminder to look back to the cross where my deliverance was accomplished. It's the power of God, not the power of self.

Temptation is the flesh calling for me to take my eyes off of Christ and to look to something else. It could be desires, negativism, pride, or anything other than Christ. Repentance is God's call for me to take my eyes off everything else but Christ. Turn to Him and receive His power to overcome.

This is where the moment of decision arises. My flesh calls me to submit my mind back under its power, but God's Spirit of wisdom says, "Turn to Me." Look at the call of God's wisdom in **Proverbs 1:**

20 Wisdom calls aloud outside; She raises her voice
in the open squares.
22 "How long, you simple ones, will you love
simplicity? For scorners delight in their scorning,
And fools hate knowledge.
23 Turn at my rebuke; Surely I will pour out my
spirit on you; I will make my words known to you.

Do you realize the power of this promise? "Turn at my rebuke...and I will pour out my spirit on you." What is the rebuke of wisdom? You are doing things your way, and God is calling you to turn to Him and follow the Spirit.

Stop and look at your life. Are your ways working? When you blow up in anger, does it accomplish good? Does brooding and cultivating frustration produce any good fruit in your heart or life? It will always do the opposite. It produces more anger, more frustration, and more pain.

You may say, "I can't overcome these things." Welcome to the club. I said the same thing, but for most of my life I missed the point. Turn at God's rebuke and He will pour out His spirit upon you. His power is your strength to overcome.

The fool hates knowledge. Such was I. Perhaps this also applies to you. How so? When God reveals the knowledge to overcome, and we choose our own ways, it is a rejection of knowledge. When you begin responding to God's call, you won't understand how any of this will work, and that's okay. The promise also is, "I will make my words known to you." It isn't until you believe God and turn to Him by faith that you begin to understand. The call comes first, we then believe and respond or disbelieve and reject. If we respond and turn to wisdom, understanding will follow. It may not be an instant understanding, but as we put our trust in God's ways, understanding will begin to dawn in our hearts.

Let me reiterate what I mentioned earlier. When you are in the heat of passion – whether that be anger, jealousy, lust, bitterness, etc. – you will not want to turn toward the call of wisdom. At least not until you begin to mature in these ways. Your desire will first be to give yourself over to anger, frustration, bitterness, and selfish brooding. God calls, but so does the flesh. When you answer God, surely He will pour out His Spirit upon you and the flesh no longer has power over your mind or life. Yet, if you reject that call, you are sowing the things which bring future consequences.

Remember when we read that God isn't snubbed? What we sow into our lives we will reap. This is also reiterated in this instruction in **Proverbs 1**. Let's continue to read:

24 Because I have called and you refused, I have stretched out my hand and no one regarded,

25 Because you disdained all my counsel, And would have none of my rebuke,

26 I also will laugh at your calamity; I will mock

when your terror comes,

27 When your terror comes like a storm, And your destruction comes like a whirlwind, When distress and anguish come upon you.

28 "Then they will call on me, but I will not answer; They will seek me diligently, but they will not find me.

29 Because they hated knowledge And did not choose the fear of the LORD,

30 They would have none of my counsel *And* despised my every rebuke.

31 Therefore they shall eat the fruit of their own way, And be filled to the full with their own fancies.

Now is the day to turn to the right way. Don't wait until you want deliverance from the consequences.

This is a hard teaching. However, this passage is not saying we can never have mercy again. I can speak from my own experiences that indeed we can turn and find deliverance. This passage is warning that there are consequences. If someone warns me that putting my hand in a fire will burn me, and I ignore the warning, will I get burned? Certainly. When burned, if I repent, will I still have blisters? You bet I will.

This is also true when it comes to wisdom's call. It especially applies to our discussion on emotions. If God warns that if we submit ourselves to anger, bitterness, and other things of the flesh we will have consequences, but we choose to do so anyway, what will happen? God's warning will be true. At some point we may recognize the consequences of our actions and look to the Lord for deliverance.

While He will fulfill His promises when we respond by faith, He does not promise to remove the consequences. But this does not mean He doesn't show us mercy and receive us into His arms. In fact, He will be our strength as we work through the consequences.

A raging man may allow his temper to control him and do violence. I've done prison ministry and met many such men. Some are in for murder, some assault, and many other crimes done through uncontrolled passion. Some of these men are truly sorry for their actions and are making a sincere change. However, they will still pay the consequences for their sins.

I watched a show where a news station worked with police to set up a sting to capture people seeking underage relationships. I watched this show as dozens of men were arrested. In the interrogation room, three of these men revealed they were Christians. All three said something to the effect of, "Something kept telling me, don't do it. Don't go. But I didn't listen."

That was the voice of wisdom. Now they are all repentant, but not one of them escaped justice. If they had turned at Wisdom's rebuke, they would have escaped, yet because they refused, they will all eat the fruit of their own way. God forgives their sin, but does not negate the consequences of their actions.

The same is true for you. When your passions rise up and call you to obey, you will also hear the call of wisdom. If you turn, God promises to empower you by His Spirit. Turning is not merely resisting, for then you are still in the flesh. The flesh profits nothing and you can't overcome the flesh with mere human effort.

Turning means you turn your heart and mind to the cross, believe God's word, which promises you have been delivered and your flesh has been put to death with its passions and desires, and receive God's spirit of deliverance by faith.

Begin cultivating a heart of faith now. What you sow, you will reap. Sow the word into your life by reading and studying the word. Sow through praying in the Spirit. Sow by setting your heart on the things above, not on the things of this world. Sow by thinking upon these things: things that are true, noble, just, pure, lovely, of good report, of virtue, and are praiseworthy. Let's again review the promise found in **Philippians 4:7**

> And the peace of God, which surpasses all
> understanding, will guard your hearts and minds
> through Christ Jesus.

Guarding your heart and mind is not your role. It is God who promises to be your guard and the provider of peace. If you do these things, God will fulfill His promises. If you sow in the Spirit, you will reap these things of the Spirit. Cultivate the good things of God in your heart and your emotions will then be built on that foundation.

Don't build your life upon emotions, but build emotions upon a Spirit filled life.

This is God's will and desire for you. Live by Wisdom's call and be abundantly blessed!

# Life Applications

- Memorize Galatians 5:8
- Think upon the call of wisdom. In what ways do you feel God is calling you to change?
- Determine to turn from your negative behaviors as you turn toward God for strength.
- Decide now that if you catch yourself acting out in negative ways, you'll stop yourself - even if you are in mid-sentence or in the middle of the action.
- Read through Proverbs 1 each day for the next week.
- Review the previous Life Applications.

# Preparing to Face the Challenge

The battle to control emotions isn't won at the time of conflict, but right now. By conflict, I mean your internal struggle. External circumstances may be the catalyst, but the real conflict is first fought inside, and you either are overcome by or gain control over your emotions.

The internal struggle may seem like a flash reaction, but control is either surrendered or gained in that instant. Your battle could be with anger, fear, jealousy, or any other thing that challenges for control. The moment of decision is just that – a moment. Therefore, you need to prepare now so you can have the right mind-set when the time comes.

Let's use anger as an example. Consider this scenario:

Jane walks in the room and sees her daughter reading a novel. "Is your homework done?" she asks.

"I forgot."

"How could you forget? You know what you're supposed to be doing. We go through this every day."

"You always start yelling at me."

Jane tries to mask her frustration, but can't keep a higher pitch from slipping into her voice. "I'm not yelling."

"You're yelling at me now. I wasn't doing anything wrong."

"I told you to do your schoolwork. You disobeyed me. That's wrong." The daughter rolls her eyes, amplifying Jane's frustration. "Don't you roll your eyes at me. I'm your mother!"

The situation escalates rapidly. The daughter argues; Jane argues. Jane shouts that she shouldn't be arguing with her parents, while the daughter shouts that she feels mistreated. When her daughter says something like, 'I hate you', or 'you hate me', things are plunged into a free-for-all. Jane screeches at her daughter, her daughter screeches at Jane. By the time the dispute ends, both sides are mentally frazzled and stressed. The original problem has been lost in the cloud of conflict. Jane's remaining day will be on edge.

Stress hasn't been relieved by the blow up. Instead, it has been amplified.

Jane readily admits she has a temper problem, but try as she might, she can't control it. For a few moments at the beginning of the conflict, she thought about her need to control her emotions. Everyday seems to be filled with conflict and each day seems to get worse. At least her nerves are getting worse.

It's not only anger that could fit into this situation. It could be jealousy, fear, or any other emotional response that builds stress or harms relationships.

Let's go back and look at Jane's breaking point – the point where she lost her cool. Voices are raising, but Jane hasn't yet lost her temper. She feels the pressure building, but the safety valves haven't yet blown off. Her daughter can't see her own lack of responsibility, and Jane is trying to explain this to her. The daughter isn't listening, she's preparing for a counterattack. They go back and forth until the daughter decides to push Jane's self-destruction button. The child knows where that button is. Or it could be many buttons. She knows what offends or hurts Jane, and when the child sees she is losing the battle, she falls back to the Nuclear Option.

If Jane has a weight problem, the nuclear option could be, "If you'd spend less time pigging out on chips and cake, maybe you wouldn't feel so bad about yourself, and people will like you." She might choose to zero in on Jane's divorce and offer her versions of the reason why dad left her mother. The target of the nuclear option could be anything, but it is guaranteed that it will be disrespectful and hurtful.

Jane's reaction is immediate. No longer is she thinking calmly. The button has been pressed and we have liftoff. "I am your mother," Jane seethes. Then she shrieks, "How dare you talk to me that way." Jane now launches her nuclear counterattack. All-out war has begun and there will be no winners.

Let's stop for a moment and examine this scenario. In an argument, both sides are trying to get the upper hand. Oftentimes, the catalyst for the argument is petty. The main focus is on gaining control. While Jane may have originally intended to resolve a small problem, within a few words, the focus has shifted from the problem to regaining power. Jane isn't trying to gain control of herself, but instead is trying to control her daughter.

The reality of human interaction is that no relationship can be healthy when one side is trying to control the other. Jane must first learn to control herself and then take steps to mature her daughter into self-control as well. Sometimes people are simply immature and unwilling to control their actions or do what is right. When our responsibility is to lead others, we may indeed have to force them to do what they are resistant to do. Even so, we must first control our reactions before we can have any hope of effectively communicating with others.

What could Jane have done to stop herself from losing control during this argument?

That was a trick question. War is not the time to strategize. Nor is the heat of an argument the time to plan your emotional response. The battle isn't won during the conflict. The battle is won or lost right now, when you have a cool head and a clear mind. Jane had already lost the battle with her emotions before she said, "Why aren't you doing your homework?"

Jane needs a new game plan. One thing is certain – her current reactions and counter-reactions are not working. They haven't worked for years. The only solution she has considered is forcing the same reactions into the argument with more volume and frustration. Because Jane hasn't considered a better course of action, she applies the same methods to the same situations. She reacts rather than responds.

A reaction is an automatic action without reasoning through a situation. A response is when we consider our options and decide on a reasonable course of action. A reaction isn't controlled. A response is.

Applying more passion and trying harder to make a solution work isn't effective. If shouting doesn't resolve the problem, shouting louder won't either. Even if you win the battle, it's a losing victory. Jane is emotionally exhausted, her daughter is emotionally exhausted, and their relationship will continue to build stress in both of their lives.

The same scenario may apply to a husband, wife, sibling, co-worker, parent, in-laws, or any other relationship you are dealing with. When your current solution isn't working, forcing it with bigger emotions won't improve your odds of success. Quite the opposite. It guarantees failure.

When a square peg doesn't fit into a round hole, does applying more force make it fit better? What about getting a bigger hammer? If you have a big enough hammer, you might be able to force the peg in, but not without destroying the peg, the hole, or both.

So why do we keep trying the same failing methods and growing more frustrated by the lack of results? We do this because we don't have any other solutions. Jane doesn't know what to do, so her frustration grows and she is now driven by the passions born through anger and not a passion for doing the right thing. And to make matters worse, Jane believes she is doing the right thing. Just because her daughter is wrong, doesn't make Jane's reaction right.

What is the solution? Admittedly, this is a difficult one to apply, but I assure you this will work. The reason solving the problem is so difficult is because we must first battle our own emotions before we can address the problem causing our grief. It's a war on two fronts. The hardest battle is our internal one. Once we master our emotions, we can see clearly to address the problem that grates on our emotions. Consider the words of Jesus in **Matthew 7:3-5**

3 "And why do you look at the speck in your brother's eye, but do not consider the plank in your own eye?

⁴ "Or how can you say to your brother, 'Let me remove the speck from your eye'; and look, a plank *is* in your own eye?

⁵ "Hypocrite! First remove the plank from your own eye, and then you will see clearly to remove the speck from your brother's eye.

Notice Jesus did not say we aren't to worry about the speck in our brother's eye. He said we must do something with ourselves first so we can see clearly to handle the situation. Stress and out of control emotions often are planks in our own eyes. The problem we are addressing is the speck.

Think back at the homework situation. Is this a big problem, or a small one? It's a small speck of a problem that should have an easy resolution. The problem is only big because of the emotions added into the mix.

Jesus intentionally used an illustration that is exaggerated to the point of absurdity. Yet this is an accurate view of what we are doing in our daily human interactions.

The person with the speck in their eye bothers us. We see something wrong which needs to be fixed. It's a real problem and is something that truly needs to be resolved. But we can't fix it. The reason? Every time we step close enough to deal with the problem, the huge board in our eye bangs around and creates more problems. We can't reach the speck. In fact, our plank is causing more damage than the speck ever could.

When we try to zero in on the speck, the plank blocks our view and the closer we get to the problem, the less we can see. Our plank dominates the situation, and soon it becomes the problem that overshadows the speck.

Isn't this a great illustration of our emotional reactions? How many times have we lost sight of the real problem and began focusing on feelings and reactions on both sides? After a heated dispute, neither party cares about the speck. Instead, one side is saying "you hate me," and the other side is saying, "You are so disrespectful." One says, "You always," the other says, "You never." By the time the dispute runs its course, neither side is satisfied and neither party cares about the speck of a problem that began the dispute. The beam is all they see.

Remember our discussion of Cain's anger in a previous chapter? When Cain became angry with his brother, Abel, what was the Lord's warning? God warned him about his anger by saying, "Sin crouches at the door. Its desire is for you, but you should rule over it." Cain chose to allow himself to be ruled by his emotions and the results were disastrous.

When emotions rule, it is always a recipe for disaster. We were not created to be ruled by our emotions. Someone is going to get hurt when we allow emotions to become the driving force in our lives. More times than not, the damage begins with you and then spreads out to those around you. There is a lot of turmoil inside before the symptoms bubble to the surface for others to see. By the time emotional problems are visible, much internal damage has already been done.

Emotional wounds are the hardest to heal. The Proverbs teach, "A brother offended is harder to be won than a city." A city can be conquered, but no one's heart can be won by force. Fortunately, emotional wounds can be healed, but not by brute force.

Healing comes through nurturing. Scars may remain, but we have constructive ways of dealing with them. In fact, a scar can become a blessing and a trophy of grace, but only after the wound has been healed. The first step in healing is to learn to deal with your emotions in healthy ways.

Let's go back to our argument with Jane and her daughter. How can Jane learn to deal with her own emotions so she can handle the situation better? Should she ignore the problem? No. It is a problem that needs to be addressed. It's a speck that needs to be removed. What will happen if we leave a speck of debris in our eye? It creates more problems, possibly an infection, and many bad things can happen from there. The speck needs to be removed, but not until Jane can get the plank out of the way. It is doing more damage than the speck, and the real problem can't be addressed until the plank is gone. Jane needs to reevaluate her own reactions prior to addressing any problem.

To illustrate this, I'm going to use my own life. I've gone through this very thing. This is why I know the solution works. It is not an easy fix, but it is very much possible to overcome our emotions and regain control of our life. Not many people know this, but I'll share my own personal confession with you.

I had a serious temper problem and I couldn't see it. The real irony is that before I married, I was known as even tempered and laid-back. It wasn't until I had to share my life with someone that these hidden flaws began to emerge. Let me first tell the story from the perspective I had at the time.

There would be times when life began closing in on me. Job stresses, tight money, too many home duties, and my wife's complaints would all hit me at one time. I literally felt like the entire world was caving in on top of me. Then my wife would add the final weight that pushed me to the breaking point. She would complain about something, I didn't want to be bothered with another issue, and she would keep pressing. I'd send out warning flares, but she never seemed to respond to them. The weight of everything became unbearable and I'd finally explode. Though I never physically hurt my wife, I would beat her back with angry words and my huge explosion of rage. I would get in her face and bully her into submission.

After the explosion, I felt a sense of relief. The weight of everything was off my back for a moment and I'd be back to my normal self in no time. Then I'd act as if nothing was wrong; however, my wife would be reeling from my reaction. In my mind, everything was justified. I tried to warn her, but she wouldn't listen. She kept pressing even though I was getting to my breaking point. To me, this was a self-preservation measure. What I didn't understand at the time was that each time I lost control, it made it harder to be in control the next time. The more I lost my temper, the more little things created stress in my life. I was giving myself over to emotions. My blowups became a constant occurrence and increased in frequency.

One day I had someone get angry with me. The issue was petty, but the person got in my face. Amazingly, I held my own temper and removed myself from the conflict. I was boiling inside, but I didn't allow it to show. In the car on the way home, I told my wife, "There is nothing worse than having someone in your face and yelling." As I spoke, I realized I had just hung myself with my own words. In that instant, my eyes were opened and I realized I had more guilt than the person I was complaining about.

Until this day, I never recognized my own temper problem. I had blinded myself to my own faults and instead blamed others for making me angry. Never mind that I was dropping a nuclear bomb on my wife for firing a cap gun.

Not only was I failing to exercise self-control, but I was using unjustifiable verbal force to bully my wife to get my way. I had never felt more convicted in my life. I determined that day to never get in her face again, and to get my temper under control. Not getting in her face was the easy part, but regaining control of my temper was not. I had allowed my anger to become my master and it did not want to step down from the throne of my life.

I determined two things in my heart that day. One, I would get my temper under control. Two, I would never again justify my explosions.

It wasn't long before a new situation arose where I again felt the weight of the world bearing down on me. I tried with all my might, but I quickly hit my stress limit and exploded. I failed on point one, but I kept myself accountable on point two. Once I cooled down, I apologized to my wife for my reaction. I did a lot of apologizing. I can remember walking outside to cool down and praying, "Lord, why can't I catch myself before I explode?"

One thing I quickly realized was even when I held my temper, I was only holding in the stress wanting to come out. Resisting an explosion wasn't the answer. I had to find a way to deal with my stress to relieve the pressure. After the next eruption, during my cool down period, I began analyzing my feelings. What made me angry? I knew how I felt – the world was caving in on top of me. But what was the root of the problem? I began to follow my emotions back to the first signs of stress. What made me feel stressful?

I made an amazing discovery about myself. I was selfish. Shocking, I know. Almost without exception, my reaction was caused by my inability to order the world the way I wanted it to be. I thought something should be done one way, but my wife saw things differently. And did things differently. The root of the problem was that I wanted to control everything and everyone to fit my self-centered world view.

When I looked at the root of the problem, it was an emotional reaction to unfulfilled selfishness. None of the things bothering me truly mattered. I was making my desires the standard of right and wrong.

It has been about eighteen years and I don't remember the specifics of our arguments, so I'll just use an absurd example that is a fairly common issue. I've seen people argue while loading the dishwasher. Some want bowls on top; the other wants bowls on the bottom. Some want to rinse all the food off before loading; the other leaves residue on the dish.

It was these types of petty issues which caused most of my stress. Granted, some of my stress came from work and the challenges of life that can't be controlled, but the catalyst for my rage were things I felt I could control. My wife wanted me to take out the garbage now; I wanted to do it later. She then complained about the smell; I complained I was in the middle of something. She would come back and start again, and then we'd start bickering. As we bickered, I began to feel as if she were pressing down on me along with the rest of the world.

In truth, I wanted a world centered upon myself. If I didn't want it, I shouldn't be forced to do it. If I wanted to do it, I shouldn't be denied. I was trying to keep everything within the boundaries of my self-centered world view. As things would escape the boundaries of my control, I would try to herd them back into place. The more things I had to keep under control, the more frustrated I became. The real pressure was caused by me trying to keep my world centered upon me. It was simply selfishness.

It was then I realized identifying selfishness was the first step toward changing my behavior. Because I had let myself lose control, I would often lose my temper before I could catch myself. I'd explode, calm down, analyze myself, and again realize my stress was over something petty, and I'd apologize to my wife. Then I'd lament before God as to why I couldn't stop myself and look at the heart of my situation before blowing up.

Then one day I caught myself. I felt the pressure building and I was ready to blow, but I thought about my reaction and asked myself, "Is this justified?" When I looked at the problem I realized this wasn't worthy of the emotional energy I was putting into it. This was something that truly didn't matter. Then I felt silly for being angry. I cast the selfish thought away, acknowledged everything didn't have to be my way, and the stress disappeared.

I still exploded more times than not, but I began catching myself more and more often. I would defuse the bomb and feel childish for my reaction because it was something that simply didn't matter. *Tomorrow I won't even remember this, so why am I concerning myself with little things which have no bearing on my life whatsoever?*.

Ultimately, my problem was a failure to fulfill what Jesus called one of the two greatest commandments. When asked what the greatest commandment was, Jesus said there were two. Love God with all your being was the first. The second comes out of the first – to love your neighbor as yourself. Love God with your all, and love others as yourself. I was willing to destroy others to love myself. Yet if I expressed the same love to others I wanted for myself, then I wouldn't have been putting my perceived needs over my wife and others. Without realizing it, I was learning to apply this basic command to my life.

Other than losing my selfish little world, there was no loss. And my selfish world needed to be dismantled. As I put these things away, I found that life became much happier when the world wasn't about me.

My wife never saw when I didn't explode. She only saw when I did. It was many months before she even noticed the changes in my life. In fact, she had a hard time believing I was changing. It wasn't until I began to look at life without self-centered eyes that I realized the emotional damage I had been doing to her and our marriage.

The Christian life is filled with breakthroughs. We live in ignorance and often suffer needlessly because we can't see the plain truth before us. But then God prepares our hearts, orchestrates events, and then opens our eyes. It becomes a 'wow' moment. We then pass through the hedge of our blindness and walk into the path God has revealed and discover God's life-changing truth. We only remain in failure when we refuse the revelation or are unwilling to take the steps to apply these truths to our lives.

This is what having someone get in my face did. It was a God-orchestrated event, placed at the right moment in my life to jolt my eyes open to what God was showing me. He showed me my self-created failure, but then showed me a plan of escape. He then called me to begin building my hopes around His plan instead of upon my desires. While I'm far from perfect, this part of my life is dead and buried. It is no longer mine.

Many other needs are present with me, and God reveals each stronghold of the flesh as He opens the door to freedom. That's the difference between self-abasement and conviction. Many people see their failure. They grovel in guilt and become more unstable and worse in their reactions. But conviction is sweet. It is God's revelation of a failure for the purpose of perfecting this area in our life according to His truth and His power to change us.

That's the loving patience of God. He knows our failures. He also knows our stubborn pride. Yet the Lord still shows us compassion and leads us out of failure and closer to Him. That's where success lives. It wasn't me changing myself and determining not to be angry. I couldn't restrain my anger. Part of me had to die. I didn't understand what God was doing at the time, but He was calling me to die to myself so I could experience life in Him. It is as the Apostle Paul said, "I die daily." It is daily dying to my selfish flesh so I can live for something better. This is what is taught in **Romans 6:8-14**

⁸ Now if we died with Christ, we believe that we shall also live with Him,

⁹ knowing that Christ, having been raised from the dead, dies no more. Death no longer has dominion over Him.

¹⁰ For *the death* that He died, He died to sin once for all; but *the life* that He lives, He lives to God.

¹¹ Likewise you also, reckon yourselves to be dead indeed to sin, but alive to God in Christ Jesus our Lord.

¹² Therefore do not let sin reign in your mortal body, that you should obey it in its lusts.

¹³ And do not present your members *as* instruments of unrighteousness to sin, but present yourselves to God as being alive from the dead, and your members *as* instruments of righteousness to God.

¹⁴ For sin shall not have dominion over you, for you are not under law but under grace.

In Christ we die to the flesh. How many things are in my life right now that I cannot see because of the blindness of my selfish pride? Many times since this event I have been brought to a new hedge to pass through. A hedge I didn't even know held me, but God reveals a new spiritual understanding to me, and then leads me into a new path of life. This path calls me to pass through the hedge between the selfish flesh and into a deeper walk in the Spirit.

This is exactly what God is trying to do in your life. Pray for God to open your eyes to see.

I am unable to bear the burden of seeing the vast differences between myself and Christ. If God showed me all that needed to be changed, I would be overwhelmed and would give up. He shows me one fault at a time. And with God, the fault is revealed when God is about to lead me out of it. Guilt has no role to play.

Guilt causes us to hide from God in shame. I was guilty of my sin against my family and against God; however, the Lord called me to leave the guilt, shame, and failure behind so He could draw me into the Spirit and receive the sufficiency of His power through grace. Grace is God's unearned favor toward us.

Dying to ourselves is very much a part of gaining control over our emotions. When God reveals your failure, it is a call for you to die to that part of your life. It is letting go of what is dead and to be crucified with Christ so you can walk in newness of life. And it doesn't stop with what you know you're struggling with. That is just one hedge to pass through.

Life is letting go of what is dying - self, being renewed with new life, and then purging the next selfish way of living so God can impart the next life-giving change. It is only when we are prideful that we stop growing. God wants to reveal the things He has in store for you, but this can only happen if you surrender to Him.

I must die daily. You must die daily. Today's victory will be forgotten during tomorrow's battles. The flesh will use apathy when all else fails. When you quit striving for godliness, you slowly lose ground.

God must open our eyes. And we don't even realize we are blinded to our faults. It is as Paul instructed the church, "Anyone who thinks he knows anything, knows nothing he ought to know." In other words, what you know is important and life-changing, but you haven't reached perfection and there is so much more God has yet to reveal to you. Regardless of the depth of your understanding, you are just getting started.

It is His pleasure to give you His kingdom, and this begins with conforming to the likeness of Christ. We are a long way from this standard of perfection, but that's okay. God changes us one step at a time.

When we quit seeing our need to change, pride is on the throne of our heart – regardless of how spiritual we or other people may think we are.

I'm not the same person I was in the early 90s. That's not because I became a better person. It's because part of me died. Many other parts of my old life have been put to death since then and the process still continues. Sometimes my old behaviors try to climb out of the grave, and I have to guard against them. I do so by standing upon the promise that I have been crucified with Christ and sin no longer has dominion over me. I frequently look back to the cross and remind myself and my flesh that the old man has been crucified. I have to be vigilant and watchful so I don't give power back to my flesh.

I am now a spiritual man – born of God into a new life. I could not crucify my own life. This was the work of God who took my old life and buried it with Christ, and then raised me as a new creation, born from the Spirit. But now that I am born in the Spirit, I am called to reckon my flesh dead each time it rises up. It may attempt to take over, but I turn to the cross and offer my body as a living sacrifice. My eyes remain on Christ and my flesh remains crucified. I must refuse its call to come down and regain its former dominion.

The same is true for you. You are a spiritual person. The flesh tries to rise up and regain dominion, but reckon, or account, yourself dead to the flesh but alive to Christ.

This is how you prepare for the challenges you will face. Die to yourself so God can take away what is corrupted and establish you in the next step toward perfection. Your failure is not the problem. It's resisting God's call that is the problem. When you see a failure, it is the call of God. He's about to do something spectacular, but you have to surrender your will and submit to His work.

# Life Applications

- Memorize Matthew 22:36-40
- Identify something that frequently stirs your internal frustration or builds stress.
- Think about the root of the problem. What is it that bothers you and why?
- Strategize now as to how to deal with it in a healthy way.
- The next time you get angry or frustrated, walk through your emotional reactions. Again determine what bothered you and why?
- Examine your life and determine how you can respond to problems without reacting.
- Recognize you can't control others or circumstances, but you can find strategies to respond in healthy ways.
- Pray for God to open your eyes as you seek and self-examine.
- Review previous Life Applications.

# I can't control my thoughts!

One of the most common concerns I hear are people who fear they have entertained a thought which makes them guilty of the 'unpardonable sin'. We'll talk about this scenario in a moment, but first, I want to look at why such things find their way into our minds.

Has a negative thought ever popped into your head without warning? Perhaps it's something you have struggled with, but sometimes it may be the most off the wall thought and not something you would willingly think upon. At times it comes at a moment of anger, or in a moment of temptation, or it could be something out of the blue – an idea you may be shocked would find its way in you.

Sometimes our thoughts are the result of spiritual warfare. This isn't always the case, but at times it is. Judas, one of Jesus' disciples, experienced such a thought. The Bible says the devil put it into the heart of Judas to betray Jesus. Of course, Judas never bought into Jesus' teaching, so he was already vulnerable. We can see that many evil thoughts and ideas can have their origins in demonic sources, but this is not always the case.

Let's stop for a moment and think upon this. There is a danger of going too far with this idea. Not every thought is an attack of the devil. Often, our mental process is the result of our own habits. When we dwell on anger, we will be susceptible to angry and vengeful thoughts. We can also yield our minds to the enemy by submitting ourselves to sin. This was the case with Judas.

Judas never accepted the role of being a disciple. In fact, the other apostles stated that he was greedy and a thief from the beginning (John 12:6). He was the one who kept the money for the twelve disciples and made a habit of taking money for himself. He looked at Jesus as a means of gain. His idea of ruling with Christ was based on his assumption that Jesus would be setting up an earthly kingdom.

When Jesus began foretelling of His death and crucifixion, Judas' hope of personal gain took a devastating blow. This put him into a position where he was open to temptation, and when Satan put the idea to him, Judas embraced it in his heart.

Another important thing to note is Judas was not a transformed believer. According to John 7:39, the Holy Spirit was not yet given because Jesus had not yet completed His work. This means the internal restraint and guidance of the Holy Spirit was not part of the believer's life. This is important to understand because if you are born into the Spirit by faith in Christ, the Bible says you have the Holy Spirit within you. The Holy Spirit guides you into all truth, convicts you of sin, and works to conform you to the image of Christ.[42] The Holy Spirit also seals us for God.[43]

There is no such thing as a demon possessed Christian. As Jesus said, a house cannot be divided and the Holy Spirit cannot have communion with devils. Since the Bible calls us the temple of the Holy Spirit, we cannot also be the temple of demons. This should give us some peace knowing that even when we struggle in thought, it is something we can overcome because we have the power of the Holy Spirit.

The Bible says, "Greater is He who is in you (the Holy Spirit) than he who is in the world (any spiritual force not of God)." The 'He' within you is the Spirit of God. If demons could reside in the believer, this statement from the Bible would be confusing, for how could we defeat something in the world if the spirit of the world was also inside our hearts?

Sin wars against our mind through our flesh, but God empowers us through our spirit. Therefore, when we have wicked thoughts, it is coming through our flesh and not the

---

[42] John 16:8, John 16:13, Romans 8:1-17
[43] Ephesians 4:30, 2 Corinthians 1:21-22

new spirit God has placed within us. The scriptures teach that when we are born into the Spirit, we become a new creation, born of incorruptible seed. Take a look at this passage in **1 Peter 1:23**

> Having been born again, not of corruptible seed but incorruptible, through the word of God which lives and abides forever.

Notice the word 'incorruptible'. This word means exactly what it sounds like. The spirit of new life God places within you cannot be corrupted. This means you can't be possessed, for possession is a spiritual state. Your new spirit cannot become wicked. It is incorruptible because its life is in God and not by man. Since it is from the Spirit of God and its life is in Christ, it cannot become corrupted. Period.

So where do these thoughts come from and how do they get into our minds? According to the Bible, it comes from our flesh. One day our bodies will be redeemed and we'll be like Christ in body as well as in spirit. For now, the Bible states that our bodies and all of creation groan with the desire to be redeemed at our adoption – the time when we receive our promise to be in God's presence for all eternity. Until then, we remain in a body that is still affected by sin.

Look at the words of the Apostle Paul in **Romans 7:15-23.** We've touched on this teaching a few times, but in this chapter we'll dig deeper so we can glean the truths that will empower us to overcome.

> 15 For what I am doing, I do not understand. For what I will to do, that I do not practice; but what I hate, that I do.
> 16 If, then, I do what I will not to do, I agree with the law that *it is* good.
> 17 But now, *it is* no longer I who do it, but sin that dwells in me.
> 18 For I know that in me (that is, in my flesh) nothing good dwells; for to will is present with me, but *how* to perform what is good I do not find.

¹⁹ For the good that I will *to do,* I do not do; but the evil I will not *to do,* that I practice.

²⁰ Now if I do what I will not *to do,* it is no longer I who do it, but sin that dwells in me.

²¹ I find then a law, that evil is present with me, the one who wills to do good.

²² For I delight in the law of God according to the inward man.

²³ But I see another law in my members, warring against the law of my mind, and bringing me into captivity to the law of sin which is in my members.

Notice how the Apostle Paul draws a distinction between his flesh and the goodness of God. When sin is spoken of, it is always associated with his flesh. It is within his flesh, not in his spirit – for the spirit of the believer is a new creation, given by God, and cannot be corrupted.

Do you find yourself struggling against temptation? Negative thoughts? And becoming apathetic when it comes to doing the right things you know you should do? Welcome to the club! If the Apostle Paul lamented over this struggle, we should not be surprised when we struggle.

So where do these thoughts come from? Though our spirit is redeemed and incorruptible, sin remains in our flesh. Not only is sin in our flesh, but it is warring against our minds and attempting to bring us back into captivity. It's a battle that will never end in this life – but it's a battle you can win. You do not have to surrender your mind to sinful thoughts. It is my hope you will understand how to win this battle by the end of the chapter.

# Who's driving this ship?

Are negative thoughts yours, or is it something warring against your mind? It depends on your active reasoning. If you're dwelling on something negative, it's safe to say you are the one guiding your thoughts and repentance is in order. If someone has wronged you and you are brooding with anger, then if a vengeful thought enters your mind, you are responsible for this and for your current emotional state.

People plan vengeance in order to pay back a wrong; therefore, they are submitting themselves to anger and creating the problem in their emotional state. When we catch ourselves brooding, God calls us to repent by forgiving the wrong-doer and surrendering the wrong to Him. Only God has the right to judge and only He has the right to take vengeance. As we discussed earlier, our calling is to forgive, pray for the one who wronged us, bless them, and turn our focus on the perfect will of God. He will bring good into our lives unless we choose to bring vengeance into our life instead.

If you are not brooding, thinking upon something tempting, or doing anything to set your mind upon sin, and a thought emerges from nowhere, it's safe to say this is an attack of the flesh. It may be spiritual warfare, but the war comes through the flesh, for Satan cannot attack our spirit. It is incorruptible. Satan can draw us out of walking in the Spirit and into the flesh. The flesh is his domain and this is the only place where a Christian can be defeated.

When thoughts arise, you do not have to take ownership of them. They do not belong to you unless you receive them into your heart. Let's say out of nowhere a blasphemous thought pops into your head. Have you sinned? No. Simply acknowledge this is not your thought and cast it out. When it comes back, cast it out again. Consider this passage from **2 Corinthians 10:3-5**

3 For though we walk in the flesh, we do not war according to the flesh.

4 For the weapons of our warfare *are* not carnal but mighty in God for pulling down strongholds,

5 casting down arguments and every high thing that exalts itself against the knowledge of God, bringing every thought into captivity to the obedience of Christ.

I can't control my thoughts!

This is the power given to you through the Spirit. Greater is He who is in you – the Spirit of God – than he that is in the world – anything or anyone who opposes God. Pay careful attention to the weapons of our warfare in verses 4-5. Satan attacks through the flesh, but we don't war according to the flesh. Our victory is found through the Spirit. We are attacked through the flesh, but we find victory in the Spirit. If you try to war through the flesh, you will lose.

Remember our discussion about Jane and her daughter? How was Jane trying to control the situation? By meeting her daughter's actions in the flesh with her own reaction through the flesh. Both sides lost, for you cannot defeat the flesh with the flesh. The same is true for your external and internal struggles – including your thought life.

Let's put this to the test. By using mere human effort I want you to try this experiment. Let's introduce a new superstition – lemons are evil. Lemons are so evil, even thinking upon them is an unpardonable sin. Don't think about their color. Don't allow your mind to see the lemon peel. For goodness sake, don't think about the sour taste which causes your lips to pucker and your mouth to water. If you salivate at all, you are in sin. Don't even think about the color yellow, for it might make you think about a lemon. Some people are so morally bankrupt they actually mix the sour lemon juice into water and add sugar. Do everything within your power to ignore those who add ice and talk about lemonade. That cool liquid in the mouth and cooling down your throat is not something you want to even imagine. Now suppose if you even allow your mind to think upon any of this, you're doomed to hell. Take a few minutes and concentrate on *not* thinking about lemons.

Did it work? Were you able to keep any thoughts of a lemon out of your mind? Well, it looks like we're all doomed together. If someone truly feared thinking upon something, what do you think would seep into their thoughts?

The truth is, you can't cast a thought out of your mind by determining not to think about it. In fact, the more we fear a thought, the more it will draw our attention. This is why people who fear committing the unpardonable sin suddenly have blasphemous thoughts entering their mind. The more emotions an idea generates – including fear – the more our subconscious processes kick in to explore the idea. It's a fact of our brains – like it or not. But it isn't the unpardonable sin. In fact, it most likely isn't a sin at all. We merely need to learn how to set our minds on something that doesn't feed negative ideas.

The mind is active and will naturally settle on what is demanding its attention. The same holds true for any thought. People fear when they have thought about blasphemy, lust, hatred, greed, and any number of temptations common to us all. Remember the promise of the sound mind? How does the Bible tell us to put all corruption out of our minds? We are taught to think on these things: whatever things are true, noble, just, pure, lovely, of good report, and praiseworthy.

To think upon is to consider its value, and treasure each of these things as though they are something to be cherished. Don't think on these as mere words, but what they mean and how scripture applies to our walk of faith. What is just? How are we made just? What did Christ do to make us just before God and how does this reveal the loving relationship He desires for us. Think upon these things and explore them in your mind as you let them establish you in faith.

Our minds do not operate in a vacuum. We must set our minds upon these things and then we have the promise that the peace of God will guard our hearts and minds through Christ. We aren't staring down our temptation, but turning from it and toward something pure. You will drive yourself insane trying to herd thoughts. They are like catching shadows. They remain just out of reach and impossible to grab hold of.

In truth, we aren't casting them out of our minds; we are casting them down from their place of dominance. I recapture my mind by setting my mind on things above – things eternal and godly. When negative thoughts attempt to capture my attention, I cast them down again by setting my mind on the right things again. Remember, sin dwells in our members – our body of flesh. So these things aren't going away, they are being dethroned. They lose their power and we refuse to give them heed, but don't be alarmed if you see them scurrying by from time to time.

Like rats, when the infestation is severe, it will take time to regain control, but you will see them losing power as you do the things God has revealed in His word. God does not require you to redeem your flesh, only that you account it as dead in Christ. This is done by putting off the flesh and putting on Christ. Here is how you regain control of your thoughts. Look at **Ephesians 4:22-24**

22 that you put off, concerning your former conduct, the old man which grows corrupt according to the deceitful lusts,

23 and be renewed in the spirit of your mind,

24 and that you put on the new man which was created according to God, in true righteousness and holiness.

Put off your former conduct. The old man is your flesh – the human nature that is inherited from Adam but was crucified in Christ. The nature is dead, but his deeds remain in the body. We put off the old *while* putting on the new. You can't do one without the other. None of us can put on the new man – our spirit led lifestyle – while remaining in the flesh. Nor can we put off the flesh without putting on our new nature. Life is not a vacuum. And the key to it all is constant renewal.

I can't control my thoughts!

The negative thoughts and emotions are scurrying around, looking for an opportunity to seize control, but they are cast off as we renew our minds and put on the spiritual man. The word of God renews our minds, and as we submit to the word, we are putting on the new man.

Once you put off the flesh, something will happen you probably won't expect. It will rise up and attempt to seize control. And it will do so again, and again, and again. However, as we grow in the Spirit, the flesh loses its grip on our minds. So what is difficult now will become easier as you learn how to walk in the Spirit. It won't completely go away until our transformation is completed at Christ's coming, but it will lose its strength.

The flesh will cease from being a strong bully which attacks and tries to overthrow, but instead will transform into a deceiver that tries to persuade you into partaking in a little temptation.

Don't blame the devil. The Bible says we are tempted when we are enticed by our own lusts. Temptation is not demonic forces seizing control, but the cravings of our own flesh. It only seems like an irresistible force because we have conditioned ourselves to receive temptation. But we overcome by dying daily. The diligent pursuit of living according to Christ's holiness is a lifelong process.

The flesh is very opportunistic. It will seize any opportunity, and there will be times when you'll lament along with the Apostle Paul, and wonder why you do what you know you shouldn't do, and why you don't do what you know you should. However, if you consistently apply the principles of scripture to your life, you will also rejoice as Paul did, "I thank God through Jesus Christ our Lord!" You then will also discover you have the power to serve God through your mind and deprive the flesh of its desire to control the body, which serves the law of sin.

Victory is given. We already have the victory. We just need to learn how to walk in it.

# The Unpardonable Sin

Let's talk for a moment about the dreaded 'unpardonable sin'.

As I mentioned earlier, we don't resist temptation by staring it down, but by turning our hearts to what is good. I'll share the scriptures with you that cover this in a moment, but let me say first that those who are asking such questions haven't committed the unpardonable sin. If God was so easily offended that a thought popping in our heads could condemn us to hell, we'd all be doomed.

Though I touched on this a moment ago, this is a topic many fear. It's the most common question I am asked; therefore, it is necessary to fully answer this question and relieve the fears of many.

We should take a moment to examine the sin of blasphemy and observe the difference between the condemnation of the Pharisees and the mercy given to the Apostle Paul – who was also a Pharisee. Both were blasphemers and both tried to stop Christianity. Both thought the church was evil and regarded Jesus as a deceiver. Both persecuted Christians and both had them put to death. Yet the Pharisee Paul was forgiven, but other Pharisees were warned that forgiveness was now impossible. Look at **Matthew 12:31-32**

> 31 Therefore I say to you, every sin and blasphemy will be forgiven men, but the blasphemy *against* the Spirit will not be forgiven men.
>
> 32 Anyone who speaks a word against the Son of Man, it will be forgiven him; but whoever speaks against the Holy Spirit, it will not be forgiven him, either in this age or in the *age* to come.

When Jesus uttered this warning, what was taking place? In verse 10, Jesus healed a man with a withered hand. The Pharisees raged against Him for healing on the

Sabbath, even though Jesus explained He was the Lord of the Sabbath. Their response to the miracle was to plot to destroy Jesus. He withdrew, and as was often the case, the Pharisees followed to watch Jesus, looking for something by which they could accuse Him. Verse 18 quotes a passage from Isaiah, foretelling that it would be self-evident Jesus was fulfilling the prophecy given about His ministry and life. In verse 22, the people brought a man who was demon possessed, and Jesus cast out the devil and healed the man. What did the Pharisees say? "This fellow does not cast out demons except by Beelzebub, the ruler of the demons."

The work of God was revealed directly to them in an unmistakable way. The Pharisees heard the word of God through Jesus' teaching. They saw the miracle of healing. They saw the affirmation of Him through the Old Testament scriptures, which, by the way, was their primary field of study. Finally, they saw Jesus' power over Satan revealed before their very eyes. Their response? "He has the power of Satan."

To make such a claim was to call the Holy Spirit of God the power of Satan. Did Satan heal the man's hand? Did Satan give Jesus the words of truth? Did Satan write the book of Isaiah which foretold of these events? Did Satan cast out himself?

Consider more of these things. When Jesus fed the five-thousand, the people demanded a sign from God in order to believe. Several times the leaders demanded a sign from Christ, and what did he say? "No sign will be given – except, the sign of Jonah." Just as Jonah was in the belly of the fish for three days, Jesus would be in the grave three days and would emerge.

In a parable, Jesus told about a man who died and was tormented in the flames of judgment. The man begged to go back and warn his brothers of that horrible place. He was told, "They have Moses and the prophets, let them hear them." This of course is the reference to the Old Testament scriptures. The man knew that like himself, they were ignoring the word of God, so he pleaded by saying they would believe if someone returned from the grave to warn them. But he was told, "If they won't believe Moses and the prophets (the word of God), they will not believe – even if someone were to rise from the dead."

Jesus proved this to be true twice – His own resurrection and by raising Lazarus. Lazarus was dead four days, and Jesus came and raised him from the dead. How did the Pharisees react? They plotted to put Lazarus to death, for many believed on Jesus because of the dead man's resurrection. All their efforts to stop Christ were fruitless and the Pharisees lamented how all their efforts to silence Him accomplished nothing (John 12:19).

When Jesus was crucified, the Pharisees persuaded the Roman governor to place a squadron of soldiers to guard the tomb so the disciples couldn't steal the body and claim Jesus had risen. Jesus did rise, and the Roman soldiers witnessed it. A squad of terrorized soldiers ran to the Pharisees and reported how they witnessed Jesus emerge from the tomb. What was the response of the Pharisees? They came up with an alternate story and offered to pay the soldiers money to hide the truth and spread their lie.

So you see, this was much more than a blasphemous thought popping into their heads. They fought against God, told others it was Satan's work, plotted to destroy the evidence of God's work, and lied to persuade others to disbelieve God. They knew without a doubt Jesus was who He claimed to be. They even acknowledged both the resurrection of Lazarus and the resurrection of Jesus. But their response was to destroy the work of God and hide the miracles. All of this stemmed from one thing – they resisted the Spirit of God working in their hearts. You see, we all were blasphemers before we were redeemed, but God didn't judge us for it.

The Apostle Paul blasphemed the work of God and called it evil. In Acts, Paul gives his testimony and says how he obtained orders from the priests and hunted down

Christians from city to city, captured them and brought them back to be put to death.

Not only did Paul cast his vote against God's people in their trials, but he also testifies of two practices we think of as despicable. He says he hailed people in their houses. In other words, he found out who was a Christian by giving them a Christian salutation. If they answered back, he knew they were believers and he would arrest them. It would be something like walking into a house and saying, "Blessings in the name of Jesus Christ." He was pretending to be a Christian, knowing that if they blessed back in the name of Jesus, they were followers of what he considered to be an evil cult of Christ.

The second despicable practice was that Paul said, "I compelled them to blaspheme." In other words, he used threats and punishment to force people to speak against Christ. Scourging was a common practice, so he may have had them beaten until they spoke evil against the way of faith in Christ. His goal was to utterly destroy the faith of believers, not to just punish them.

So why didn't God judge Paul as He did the other Pharisees? He also blasphemed, called the work of God evil, and set out to kill anyone who followed Jesus in order to destroy the faith. In action, there is no difference between the Apostle Paul and the Pharisees whom Jesus proclaimed, "You cannot be forgiven in this life, or the life to come." I say, no difference in action while in the act of blasphemy, but there was a huge difference when seeing the work of the Holy Spirit. Let me explain this first by looking at two passages. Look first at **Romans 1:18-19**

> 18 For the wrath of God is revealed from heaven against all ungodliness and unrighteousness of men, who <u>suppress</u> the truth in unrighteousness,
> 19 because what may be known of God <u>is manifest in them</u>, for <u>God has shown</u> *it* <u>to them</u>.

Now read **2 Thessalonians 2:10-12**

<sup>10</sup> and with all unrighteous deception among those who perish, because <u>they did not receive the love of the truth</u>, that they might be saved.

<sup>11</sup> And <u>for this reason</u> God will send them strong delusion, that they should believe the lie,

<sup>12</sup> that they all may be condemned <u>who did not believe</u> the truth <u>but had pleasure in unrighteousness</u>.

I underlined the key points I wanted you to notice. The wrath of God was revealed against the ungodly AFTER He made Himself known to them and showed the truth to them. Those who refused to receive the love of the truth were given over to the strong delusion so they will believe a lie. Why? It was for this reason – they rejected the truth that they might be saved. A truth God revealed in their heart, according to Romans 1.

Paul thought the work of God was evil and was something to be stamped out. He was wrong. He was corrupt, sinful, and a wicked man who blasphemed and forced others to blaspheme. Yet he found mercy.

The Pharisees were evil men who thought the work of God was evil. They blasphemed and encouraged others to blaspheme – even issuing ordinances that if anyone testifies to Christ, they would be permanently kicked out of the Synagogue and excluded from the Jewish culture everyone depended upon. They tried, condemned, and executed believers in Christ.

The ONLY distinction between those who received mercy, and those who received judgment is the response to the truth of God when it was revealed to their hearts by the Holy Spirit.

It is not our response to the word, but our response to the revelation of the word. There is a difference. The Bible says the natural man – those viewing the world through human nature, or the flesh – cannot receive or understand the things of God, for they are spiritually discerned. The

I can't control my thoughts!

word of God is foolishness to the flesh, and we are all born into the flesh. Hearing truth does not turn the light bulb on in our hearts. It is the Holy Spirit who opens our eyes to see the truth and then calls our hearts to respond.

Faith comes by hearing the word of God (Romans 10:17). You can hear the word of God without faith, but you cannot have faith without hearing the word of God. God calls us through the word, and He opens our understanding in His own time. This is why someone will hear the word their whole lives, and then suddenly understand the gospel and are born into the Spirit.

From the outside, you and I cannot determine what God is doing in someone's heart. Just because someone doesn't respond, does not mean they are resisting the Holy Spirit. Rejecting the truth is not what brings us under judgment. We all reject the truth in our flesh. But, when the Holy Spirit pulls back the veil of our flesh, reveals the truth to us, and makes God manifest to our heart and understanding, the moment of decision has come.

The decision is not whether we will choose God. We cannot choose God. God chooses us and calls us to Christ. The ONLY decision is whether we will resist the Spirit of grace that is being given to us.

Go back to the passages above. Those judged SUPPRESS the truth. It is taking the truth which has been revealed to our hearts, refusing it, and trying to push it away from our understanding that God condemns. It is *for this reason* we are given over to our vile passions and turned over to the lie we have already chosen.

So the problem is not blasphemy in thought, but blasphemy by resisting the Holy Spirit and turning against the truth being revealed by the hand of God. Then, and only then, have we committed the unpardonable sin. We cannot be forgiven in the life to come because we remain in our sins. We have chosen to live for the flesh and have pleasure in unrighteousness, and there is no redemption for those who die without receiving the love of the truth. For God has revealed it in them.

Inside the heart of man, God manifests Himself, calls us to lay down our lives, and offers a new life in Christ, born after the Spirit. But those condemned in the above passages, like the Pharisees, despise a God who calls them to let go of their lives in this world, and have suppressed the truth revealed in them. They reject the revelation of God in their hearts and cling to the flesh. They love a life grounded in sin and count the sacrifice of Christ as a worthless thing (Hebrews 10:29).

We all struggle with different thoughts at different times. When an offending thought pops in our head, it is not a sin. It is our flesh that has sin in its members and wars against our minds in an attempt to bring us back into its dominance.

We are commanded to guard our hearts, for out of it come the issues of life. Our minds guard our hearts. Jesus said, "Out of the heart proceed evil thoughts, murders, adultery, fornication, thefts, false witnesses, and blasphemies." It is not a sin until it proceeds from the heart. Jesus said, "A good man out of the good treasure of his heart brings forth good things, and an evil man out of the evil treasure brings forth evil things." **(Matthew 12:35)**

Notice, the heart doesn't produce these things. They are thoughts we have stored as treasures. Whether good or evil, the things in our heart are things we valued enough to store as treasures.

Let's summarize what has been discussed in this chapter. When I dwell on evil thoughts, I am treasuring those things in my heart. If I entertain thoughts of lust, I am treasuring something in my heart that will emerge in my life as sin. The same is true for hatred, greed, covetousness, blasphemy, and any other sin.

When those thoughts enter our minds, it begins as an involuntary idea. Involuntary thoughts are not sin, and we

I can't control my thoughts!

will not be held accountable for them. It's not until we welcome the thought and surrender our minds to it that it becomes sin.

There are indeed consequences when we treasure sin in our hearts, but missing out on God's forgiveness is not one of those consequences – unless we refuse God's call to let go and receive freedom. May we find confidence in the promise of **Isaiah 55:7**

> Let the wicked forsake his way, And the unrighteous man his thoughts; Let him return to the LORD, And He will have mercy on him; And to our God, For He will abundantly pardon.

Do not fear your flesh, but overcome with the power of God given to you. Have confidence in the Lord, for He has mercy, He abundantly pardons, and He becomes our sure foundation which overcomes any threat. Our weaknesses are not a hindrance to the Lord – for His strength is made perfect in our weakness.

Victory is found in surrendering to the Spirit of God.

# Life Applications

- Memorize Ephesians 4:22-24
- Set time aside each day to renew your mind through the word, prayer, and meditating upon the things God has told us to think upon.
- Daily remind yourself that harmful thoughts are not yours. Reject them and turn your mind to God's word.
- Each morning die to your will and put on the new man according to God's will.
- When you feel as though you failed or have blown it, claim the promise of Isaiah 55:7.
- Remind yourself that God doesn't judge you for who you are, but blesses you for who you will be when you stand before Him.
- Review the Life Applications from previous chapters.

# Turning Mountains into Molehills

Each person faces a twofold challenge in daily life. One is to keep ourselves from making big deals out of little problems. The second is that we learn how to positively manage big problems so they can be resolved. Problems should be resolved; they shouldn't become our barriers.

Years ago a researcher set out to understand why some people are luckier than others. He wanted to know why certain people found lucky breaks while others failed and ended up being among those counted as unlucky in life. He followed several families for many years and discovered some interesting truths.

Both lucky and unlucky people encountered similar challenges and have common hard breaks, but how people responded to adversity determined the outcome of their misfortune. Some people hit a wall, made an effort, and failed. They tossed their hands up and said, "I tried. This always happens to me."

Others hit walls, were knocked down, and refused to accept failure. The only real difference between those who found 'luck' was how they responded to adversity. The 'lucky breaks' didn't come to the most talented, the most wealthy, or the most charismatic people. The breaks came to those who persevered. Eventually, opportunity presents itself, but it is only seen by those who keep looking for the good behind every circumstance in life.

This is not to say each person faces the exact same circumstances. Some people face hardships that most others will never experience, yet even from the worst environments this truth emerges. Two people from the same difficult environment can have very different outcomes in life. Why do some people overcome the tragedies of life while others in the same environment carry failure into the next generation?

This is often seen in dysfunctional families with two or more children. Each child endures the same harsh environment, but they often have very different outcomes in life. Those who give up will never overcome challenges because they are more focused on the failures in life than the goal that lies ahead.

It's all about attitude. Not one of us can predict life and not one of us can prevent challenges, hardships, or adversities. It's coming to us all. But each person's attitude determines how they respond to it. Some people turn the slightest problem into a mountain, while others seek to climb over the mountain. There is not one person who has a bad attitude forced upon them. Quite the opposite. We force our attitudes upon every circumstance we encounter. A bad attitude inflates the mountain, while the good attitude creates expectation and hope that is bigger than the mountain.

Let's consider a few examples in the Bible. One is an example we touched on earlier – the people of the Exodus. God gave His people the promise of a land flowing with milk and honey. It was the land given to Abraham before Israel was enslaved in Egypt. Through many miracles God led the people out of bondage, defeated armies, made a way across the Red Sea, fed and watered them in the desert, and finally led them straight to the promise. In less than two weeks God's people could have been in the Promised Land.

What was God's desire? It was to give His promise to His people. And the Lord took them straight from Egypt to the edge of the promise. His promise was, "I have given you this land, I will be with you, and I will fight for you." But God tested His people with adversity. He sent twelve spies into the land, one representative from each tribe. They returned with good news and bad news. The good news, the land was just as God described it. Flowing with milk and honey, and it is a good land. They brought back many samples as proof.

But there was a problem. Adversity stood between the people and the promise. Let the spies explain the situation for themselves. Look at **Numbers 13:33**

"There we saw the giants (the descendants of Anak came from the giants); and we were like grasshoppers in our own sight, and so we were in their sight."

Notice the words they chose. We were like grasshoppers in our own sight. This is the challenge you and I face each time problems arise. Why are the problems big? Because we are looking at it through our eyes instead of the Lord's.

God destroyed the armies of Egypt, the greatest world power of that day. And He did it without a single man having to fight. Yet now they are afraid of the descendants of Anak? Anak were people of great stature. Admittedly, they were fierce looking warriors, but that was part of the test. Would God's people put their trust in adversity, or would they trust in the promises of God?

Only two men out of twelve were willing to trust the Lord, Caleb and Joshua. Everyone else went into a panic and turned from the Lord. Because they could not trust the Lord, God swore they would never receive the promise. Other than Caleb and Joshua, not one person saw the Promised Land of God. Because they trusted adversity, the Lord allowed them to choose it.

While God's plan was to lead them directly to the promise, they instead wandered forty years through the desert. Adversity was only intended to be a gravel road they had to pass over. Forty years later, Joshua proved God's original intent, for not one adversity overcame their march toward the promise. Yet an entire generation was lost because they believed the threat over the promise.

To put this in our terms, many of us trust in our problems and allow adversity to turn our hearts from the Lord. This is why few people actually experience what God has in store for them. Like the people escaping Egypt, they can see God's hand when things go perfectly, but not when they have to trust God to lead them through trouble instead of around it. The Israelites felt that God should have kept trouble away from them.

Isn't this exactly what most people live out in their lives? A problem arises and they exalt it like a mountain. In their eyes, the problem is huge and it becomes insurmountable. Instead of raising their hands to the Lord, they toss their hands up in surrender to adversity. We must learn to surrender our wills to the Lord, not surrender to our problems.

Adversity may indeed be a big problem and hard to overcome, but that's okay. God will allow problems bigger than your ability so He can reveal His power to you. It requires no faith if the solution is within our own power. It's not our battle unless we make it so. We wander through the desert of despair, while every problem weighs down upon us and we find no relief for our souls. Yet the relief is within our grasp, if we'll just take it. It's called faith in God.

Faith is believing the word of the Lord to the point where we are willing to put our trust in Him. Faith was the strength of Job. When in the midst of losing his family, possessions, and health, Job uttered the greatest testimony of faith in the Bible, "Though He slay me, yet will I trust Him."

In the end, what happened in Job's life? Though he lost much, he gained ten times more. The same is true for you and I. We often get so caught up in what we are losing that we can never receive the abundant promise of what God is giving. When we become bitter over losses, we also are turning from the Lord – who blesses those who endure with faith.

This is the reason for adversity. It's to prove what is in our hearts. Anyone can trust God when the going is easy and when we're getting what we want. But let adversity arise and let us feel threatened, and we'll reveal the truth of what is in our hearts. Adversity reveals whether we are walking by faith in the Spirit, or by the sight and strength of the flesh.

Turning Mountains into Molehills

Here's the real irony of the story of Israel's rejection of the promise. They withdrew from the Lord because they viewed the giants of Anak as too strong for them. Yet Caleb entered the land as an eighty-five year old man. When they were dividing the inheritance, Caleb requested the mountains where He would feel closer to the Lord. Do you know who inhabited the mountains? Yes. The giants of Anak. Caleb, the oldest man in Israel said, "The Lord will drive them out before me." He knew they could not stand, and sure enough, he drove them out.

Caleb and Joshua endured the adversities of the desert for forty years while waiting for the promise. Not one time do we see these two men complaining. They patiently waited because at the time God swore that not one of their peers would enter the promise, He also promised they would. They endured in faith, because the promise was real. Look at the words of **Hebrews 10:38**

Now the just shall live by faith; But if *anyone* draws back, My soul has no pleasure in him."

It's God's good pleasure to give you His kingdom, but this is a call to receive it by faith. Those who draw back miss the pleasure of God's blessing toward them. The opposite is true for those who don't draw back. The same Lord who made the above statement also said, "This is the victory that overcomes the world – our faith."

Like the example of Joshua and Caleb, when we walk in God's purposes by faith, adversity will arise, but nothing can stand against God's will. We then will walk in the victory that overcomes the world – our faith in God.

Faith is believing God. Not just intellectually, but actively. It's the person who is willing to put God's word to the test and live by it – even in adversity or temptation. We endure because of the joy set before us. This joy is grounded in the promises of God.

The heart which is grounded in the word of the Lord cannot be moved; however, the mountain can be. Look at the promise Christ gave in **Matthew 21:21-22**

> 21 So Jesus answered and said to them, "Assuredly, I say to you, if you have faith and do not doubt, you will not only do what was done to the fig tree, but also if you say to this mountain, 'Be removed and be cast into the sea,' it will be done.
> 22 "And whatever things you ask in prayer, believing, you will receive."

Jesus again used another variation of this teaching in **Luke 17:6**

> So the Lord said, "If you have faith as a mustard seed, you can say to this mulberry tree, 'Be pulled up by the roots and be planted in the sea,' and it would obey you.

Notice how both of these examples focused on immovable objects. Try plucking up a tree and see what happens. It doesn't budge. The strongest man on earth couldn't take the trunk of a grown mulberry tree and rip it from the ground, much less cast it anywhere.

Stand before the mountain of adversity. Can you move it? No. And it isn't your job to move it. God doesn't call you to move mountains; He calls you to have faith in His ability to move mountains. It's not about believing in yourself. You are limited to your own strengths, weaknesses, and limitations. It's about trusting in the Lord, for according to Jesus, what is impossible with men is possible with God.

We are not called to speak our will to the mountains. We are called to walk in God's will and conquer the mountain. The promise is that if God calls us to move an immovable object, it cannot stand if we are walking according to His will. When something stands like a mountain between us and fulfilling God's calling, we must refuse to consider its strength. We rebuke the challenger of

Turning Mountains into Molehills

God's will by declaring God's purposes and walking where He has called us to walk. We may say, "Be removed," but unless it's an answer to God's call, we aren't promised the power to remove the mountain.

This isn't a promise for us to have the power to fulfill our selfish will, but the promise that if we are walking in God's purposes, nothing can thwart His will. At times, the Lord will allow you to struggle. This is where faithfulness separates the believer from the one who feels inspired, but continues to live according to the flesh.

The challenger might be a valley, mountain, the gates of hell, your internal struggles, or any other thing. These may have the power to stand against human abilities, but they cannot prevent God's hand. If you know God's purpose for you (and you will if you practice living out the things we've discussed so far), then the mountain serves no other purpose than to test you to see if you believe the flesh, or believe the word of God.

Don't forget the promise, "I can do all things through Christ who strengthens me." Do not reverse this. It isn't Christ who does all things through us, but we do His will through Him. We are not asking God to enter into our plans to fulfill our purposes. We are submitting to His purposes and entering into His work.[44] When we are in Christ and walking in God's will, His strength is perfected in our weaknesses. We then have no limitations in Him. You have limitations, but the Lord will complete His plan – and there are no limitations.

While the faithless person turns molehills into mountains, and views them as giants in their own eyes, God is calling us to say to the mountains, "Be removed and cast into the sea." Think of the weight of this truth.

Unbelief exalts molehills into mountains that defeat us, while faith is the victory that overcomes the world. Through faith, not only are we not exalting the molehills, but we are

---

[44] Ephesians 2:10

casting down the mountains. We do so because faith is not in our efforts or our selfish will, but it is in the Lord's work within us that calls us to walk in the works He prepared beforehand.[45]

When we are pursuing the purpose of our calling, things will stand in our way. This is assuming we are living according to His purposes. A life without direction is a barrier in itself. But when we see the glory of God's purpose in our lives, we will also hear the calling to come and follow. But the Lord will allow things to test us and challenge us. This is why we are promised all the good things of His kingdom if we overcome. "To Him who overcomes, I will grant to sit with Me on My throne." All the greatest promises are to those who overcome.

We overcome our will first, and then we overcome anything that stands in our way of fulfilling God's call. Fear, frustration, guilt, greed, lust, adversity, and many other struggles will stand as trees and mountains in your way. But as Jesus said, "Be of good cheer, I have overcome the world."

Through His overcoming, we are also given the faith that overcomes the world.

---

[45] Ephesians 2:10

Turning Mountains into Molehills

# Life Applications

- Memorize Ephesians 6:5-8.
- How does this passage apply to your life today? How does this principle apply to your career, home life, and responsibilities?
- Come up with a plan now for how you will respond on your job and other responsibilities.
- How will your positive attitude affect your work and the things you dislike or feel is unfair?
- According to the passage above, what happens when you serve with a good attitude?
- Will the end result be fair?
- What will be the result if you adopt a negative attitude?
- Read Hebrews 10:38. What happens when you allow your heart to draw back from God? What happens to the person who does not draw back, but endures regardless of circumstances?
- Is it possible to live for your purposes and have confidence when adversity blocks your way?
- Evaluate your life and look for areas that need to be surrendered to the will of God.
- Take time to review Life Applications from previous chapters.

# Give the Lord no rest

**Isaiah 62:6-7**

6 I have set watchmen on your walls, O Jerusalem; They shall never hold their peace day or night. You who make mention of the LORD, do not keep silent, 7 And give Him no rest till He establishes And till He makes Jerusalem a praise in the earth.

Though I've read this passage many times, I recently reread it and the passage stood out as one which truly applies to this book. Though this scripture is directed at Israel, the principle applies also to the church and your individual life.

What stands out the most is the Lord is the one speaking in this passage. God set up the watchmen and God called His people to prayer. He then instructed them to give Himself no rest until their prayers were answered.

God wants you to persistently pursue what is right in prayer. Not only to pursue, but to give the Lord no rest until He fulfills the burden He has laid on your heart. If you feel the need, it may be that God has called you to be a watchman. When God stirs His people with a burden to pray, it's because He intends to do something in their midst. But His first instruction is to call out men and women who He can prove to be faithful.

The call to prayer is a call of faithfulness. One thing God requires is that we be found faithful. (1 Corinthians 4:2) The Lord shows Himself strong on behalf of those whose hearts are completely His.[46] Those who are seeking Him with their whole heart are the ones who give Him no rest, but consistently go before His throne of grace until He answers.

God knows what He intends to do, but He chooses to prove our hearts before doing His greatest work through us.

---

[46] 2 Chronicles 16:9

The Bible warns that we must ask in faith, pursuing the Lord without doubt. The Bible calls those who cast a prayer out and then give up – a double-minded person. Like the waves of the sea, they are tossed back and forth by emotions and circumstances. To this type of person God has declared, "Let not that man suppose he will receive anything from the Lord." (James 1:7)

The prayer of faith is to long so deeply for the will of God that we pursue His heart to find it. And then we will receive it. The prayer is not a desire of self-gratification. My blessings are fulfilled in His promises. There's no need to pursue my desires for things and benefits through selfish prayers. God has already promised to bless those who are faithful.

God blesses the faithful, not the selfish beggar.

God reveals a need. The need is often something we must have or must do in order to accomplish His will. Or it could be a prayer to remove barriers which distract us from that will. He then calls us to pursue His will by faith, and to pray without ceasing. To pray without ceasing does not mean we pray nonstop, but that we consistently set ourselves aside for prayer while diligently seeking His will. It's also to have a constant communion with God in spiritual fellowship.

We should always be in communion with God, even if we are not in our dedicated prayer time.

Let's go back to our passage in Isaiah 62 that introduced this chapter. The call of faith begins with God declaring His will – to establish Jerusalem in righteousness, make her a light to the nations, and be a crown to the Lord. He promised not to forsake her, but to establish her on the foundation of the Lord. He then called His people to believe this promise and pursue it. When God's people had the heart to pray without ceasing and refuse to abandon the promise (even though the city was in ruins), then they were in a spiritual condition to be a part of God's plan. Only then did He step in and fulfill His promise.

This is praying in faith. It is to capture a glimpse of God's will through His word, and pursue it without accepting anything short of what the Lord has revealed. It is to seek without giving up. Consider the words of Jesus in **Matthew 7:7-11**

> 7 " Ask, and it will be given to you; seek, and you will find; knock, and it will be opened to you.
>
> 8 "For everyone who asks receives, and he who seeks finds, and to him who knocks it will be opened.
>
> 9 "Or what man is there among you who, if his son asks for bread, will give him a stone?
>
> 10 "Or if he asks for a fish, will he give him a serpent?
>
> 11 "If you then, being evil, know how to give good gifts to your children, how much more will your Father who is in heaven give good things to those who ask Him!

We must first learn what God considers good. While God often blesses us in ways we find gratifying, that which is truly good is something that either meets a need or has eternal significance.

Also, a little has been lost in translation from Greek to English in the above scripture. To knock isn't just to knock and quit. It's the act of knocking. It is to knock and keep on knocking. Seek and keep on seeking. It's to ask and keep on asking. It is to give the Lord no rest until He fulfills the burden of our heart. A burden He gave us.

This is also why faith must be something we build our lives upon. We don't supplement our lives with a little God time, but we lay down our lives so we can live in the Spirit and see His revelation to us. A self-centered life is blind to the secret counsel of God.[47] Prayer is founded upon a life built on faith, and faith comes from the Lord and His word.

---

[47] Proverbs 3:32

Give the Lord no Rest

The prayer of faith will be answered, for if we ask anything according to His will, He hears and grants our petition.[48]

There is no greater joy than to pursue the heart of God, pray without ceasing, and give Him no rest until the purpose He has revealed is fulfilled. It is God who commanded us to pray and give Him no rest. He delights in the heart that seeks Him and pursues without ceasing. Consider **Psalm 119:2-4**

2 Blessed *are* those who keep His testimonies, Who seek Him with the whole heart!

3 They also do no iniquity; They walk in His ways.

4 You have commanded *us* To keep Your precepts diligently.

Seeking Him with all our heart is how we keep our hearts from iniquity, and how we learn to walk in His ways. This is where the blessings of God are discovered. Seek the Lord. Give Him no rest from your prayers.

This is what our focus should be upon. If we are spinning our wheels on personal crises, it shows that our eyes are on the molehills and mountains and not on the Lord. With the Lord, every mountain will be made low and every path straight. But this comes after we have been tested and have learned to place our hearts on the eternal things of God, and not our flesh's demand for comfort and gratification.

Trouble will come. Adversity will come. However, the Lord is our refuge, the one who renews, delivers, and rewards. In Him is your reward. Whether we think something is a blessing or not, anything that takes our focus off Him is a distraction.

Don't let your molehills become mountains and don't let your mountains turn you away from faith. Let's conclude this chapter with the words of **Habakkuk 3:17-19**

---

[48] 1 John 5:14-14

<sup>17</sup> Though the fig tree may not blossom, Nor fruit be on the vines; Though the labor of the olive may fail, And the fields yield no food; Though the flock may be cut off from the fold, And there be no herd in the stalls --

<sup>18</sup> Yet I will rejoice in the LORD, I will joy in the God of my salvation.

<sup>19</sup> The LORD God is my strength; He will make my feet like deer's *feet,* And He will make me walk on my high hills.

Notice that joy doesn't exist because of the absence of adversity. It is our expression of faith and gratitude to God, even in the midst of trials. The Lord inhabits the praise of His people; therefore, a heart of praise will experience God in the midst of any circumstance. Then our faithfulness will be tested and proven worthy of God's promises. He sustains any who turn to Him as their strength. Thanksgiving overrides our negative emotions.

A heart of faith, grounded in the word of God, will turn mountains into molehills. Exalt the Lord, not your circumstances. Then He will reward and sustain you. Praise and thankfulness are acts of faith. It is the evidence of a heart that trusts in the Lord.

The person who believes the Lord will be the one who perseveres – regardless of circumstances. This is what it means to be an overcomer.

Seek the Lord so He can reveal His calling over your life. Maintain an attitude of praise and pray for God to complete His will in your life and in the church. Then give Him no rest until He accomplishes the burden and hope of your heart.

Know Him and then you will know His heart and hear the call of prayer.

# Life Applications

- Memorize 1 John 5:14-15.
- Read James 4:3. What types of prayers does God answer?
- Read Hebrews 11:6. Who finds the rewards of God?
- Read Genesis 15:1. What is the great reward promised to those who walk by faith?
- Read Matthew 6:33. How do we claim the promises of God?
- Ask God to give you a seeking heart.
- Ask God to call you out of self-centered religion.
- Ask God to reveal the things He is calling you to join in His labors to accomplish.
- Pray until you see His work accomplished in your heart first, and then in the calling of your life.
- Review Life Applications from previous chapters.

# Setting Our Emotional Table

Every day we set the table for the emotions that feed our attitude. We either dine on positive or negative emotions. Either we determine that we'll face life with a bad attitude or a good one. Do you feast off a positive attitude? Or dumpster dive into negative emotions?

Each of us sets the stage for how we respond to each situation by our attitudes. Do you begin a task with grumbling about everything you don't like? Does the day begin by murmuring and complaining? How much joy do you think this is going to create in your life? A negative attitude does not change any circumstance; it merely makes it harder to bear.

Life is filled with things we don't like and situations we'd rather not have to deal with. When approaching a difficulty with a good attitude, the results are much more likely to have a good outcome. If we approach life with a negative attitude, negative results will follow. Even if there is a successful outcome, there will still be little joy or satisfaction. A poor mind-set blinds us to the good we can glean from every situation.

Not one of us can eliminate unwanted circumstances that arise in life. None of us can avoid the tough breaks. We all have to do things we don't enjoy – and sometimes we have to do the things we hate. Though we can't avoid problems in life, every one of us can control how we approach them.

Life isn't fair, but this doesn't mean we are destined to an unfair outcome. A bad attitude always makes unwanted situations worse. It never makes it better. Let me repeat this. A bad attitude never once made anything in anyone's life better.

The same cannot be said about a good attitude. A good attitude enables us to make the most out of every situation – whether it be good or bad. Consider your job. Whether you are a homemaker or labor in the workforce, daily you are faced with tasks you do not like doing. These are tasks which must be handled whether we complain our way through, or make the best of a bad situation. A grumbler never finds good. A complainer never sees the opportunities God hides in the crevices of difficulties. Consider the instructions of **Philippians 2:14-15**

> 14 Do all things without complaining and disputing,
> 15 that you may become blameless and harmless,
> children of God without fault in the midst of a
> crooked and perverse generation, among whom you
> shine as lights in the world,

Your good attitude shines a light in the dark world. A bad attitude joins the darkness. Not only this, but according to scripture, we are not rewarded for what we do. We are rewarded for our attitudes. The Apostle Paul explained this when he spoke about his own labors in the Lord. He explained that if he labored willingly, he had a reward from God, but if against his will, he was still required to obey.[49]

This should be self-evident. Think about parenthood. When children are given responsibilities, do they have a choice to disobey? If a parent is wise, they will not allow children to neglect their responsibilities. Otherwise children will grow up to expect this from the world. Instead, kids are given duties and they have to fulfill them. Let's consider the value of two responses.

If a child is given a task and they do it willingly, what is a parent's response? We want to give them more privileges and we can trust them to be responsible enough not to abuse privileges. If a child has to be forced into obedience, is there a reward? Does the grumbling and complaining child earn more privileges? No. If I have to spend more time managing someone than it would take for me to do it myself, why would I reward this behavior?

---

[49] 1 Corinthians 9:17

With young kids, they will spend thirty minutes lying in the floor moaning and trying to avoid a ten minute task. Not only have they lost time they could have spent doing something more enjoyable, but they still have the task waiting to be done. Their negative attitude is robbing them of the good things they want.

This applies to the life of a Christian as well. Do we really expect God to bless our lives if we are murmuring our way through every task, or resisting and complaining about what we don't like? The ones who are faithful in the little things are the ones trustworthy in the big things.[50] If we walk by faith and shine His light in our attitudes, we will experience relief from the burden of our emotions, and we'll be blessed by the Lord.

Grumbling is a lack of faith. So is complaining. A negative attitude reveals a heart that despises the life God has called us to. God tests us daily. Those who complain as if God has no right to require anything of them are rejecting the path of God that leads to, and through, the goodness of the Lord. Grumbling is a rejection of God's work in our life – for we are testifying we don't believe He is caring for us and producing good. Can I expect God to intervene on my behalf if I am fighting Him every step of the way?

Someone might say they aren't complaining against God, but this isn't so. Consider this passage in **Psalm 37:23**

The steps of a *good* man are ordered by the LORD,
And He delights in his way.

If God is directing my steps, and I am lashing out at where I am going, then I am fighting His will. Do I believe God's promise that all things work together for good? This promise is to those who are called into His purpose, who then answer this call. It isn't a promise given to those who say, "I'm going the way I want to go. God you must bless my ways."

---

[50] Luke 16:10

We've all heard it said, "Life is not fair." Is this true? Those who believe this are looking at this life as though our daily existence is all there is. But it's not.

Blessed is the person whose life is on a pilgrimage. That's the promise. If we are looking only at the 70-year human perspective, it isn't fair. Even the Apostle Paul acknowledged this when he said, "If we have hope only in this life, we are men most pitiable."[51] But our hope is eternal and our blessings are beyond comprehension. Is it fair that my life is blessed beyond my comprehension? Life is more than fair if I have eyes to see it. Consider the words of **1 Timothy 5:24-25**

[24] Some men's sins are clearly evident, preceding *them* to judgment, but those of some *men* follow later.
[25] Likewise, the good works *of some* are clearly evident, and those that are otherwise cannot be hidden.

Have you been wronged? This is not for you to be concerned about. Some sins become evident to the world, but even if they escape notice, they don't escape God's notice.

Even so, the main point I want to draw from is the second verse above. Do your works go unnoticed? All people do good things that are not noticed. This is especially true for parents and those who serve others in ministry or leadership. I once had someone quit leadership because they didn't get enough recognition. They sent me a letter complaining about all they did that no one saw. I had to resist saying, "Welcome to the club."

The truth is most of the good we do will go unnoticed. And we only notice a fraction of the good done to us. This is something every leader must realize. For one, we should become more observant to notice the efforts of others. This is an area I fall short in. We should also serve because we know our service is to the Lord and not to man.

---

[51] 1 Corinthians 15:19

If you expect kudos each time you give of yourself, you'll be disappointed often. However, if you recognize the truth that many of our works may be hidden from view, but cannot be hidden from God, we know He will be our rewarder. What's more, His reward is greater than the rewards of this life. It is as Jesus said when observing the Pharisees. They made sure everyone saw their works so they would get recognized. Jesus said, "They have their reward."

The praise of men was the only reward they could expect, for they served only to get recognized. The reward of God is greater. If He chooses to honor us in this life, fine. If not, we certainly won't be without reward in the life to come. This is true as long as our attitude is right.

Setting our emotional table is to take the time to get ourselves in the right frame of mind. Taking humility upon ourselves is part of setting the table.

If my life is driven by pride, my emotional responses will be as well. Wounded pride draws a severe response. And it often leads to bitterness and hatred. That's when we demand our own rights and demand respect. The truth is we lay down our rights before God, and respect is something that must be willingly given. It can't be demanded. Bullying someone into respect is only getting a pretentious substitute. No one respects the demander.

It's not my responsibility to defend my reputation, get recognition, or make sure I get credit for the service I do. I'm called to humble myself so that God can exalt me in due time. That time may be this life, or the life to come.

Setting our minds upward also sets our emotional table. Life doesn't appear fair if we are looking at this life as though it is the meaning of it all. But when I adopt an eternal view, petty things don't matter and wrongs don't need to be avenged. I can sacrifice when I realize the Lord repays. What can I give or lose that the Lord won't make up for in abundance?

Stepping out of the flesh and setting my mind on the Spirit is an act of faith. It sets the stage for my entire life. I endure because I believe in the joy the Lord has set before me. I am miserable when all I can see is my lack of immediate comfort or benefit. When I don't have eyes of faith, I mourn over what I have lost and forget what I am gaining.

Through faith, I see the future and the glory of the favor of God. It has already been shown toward me through Christ, I get a glimpse of it through God's promises, but one day I will see it in person. Not one of us will mourn over the things of this passing life. Nothing lost here will be our concern in eternity. That is, nothing except the rejection of God's work in our lives.

Let's conclude this chapter with a few passages from Proverbs.

**Proverbs 15:13** A merry heart makes a cheerful countenance, But by sorrow of the heart the spirit is broken.

**Proverbs 17:22** A merry heart does good, *like* medicine, But a broken spirit dries the bones.

**Proverbs 15:15** All the days of the afflicted *are* evil, But he who is of a merry heart *has* a continual feast.

It's interesting that the broken spirit comes from the heart that clings to sorrow. Have you worried yourself sick? There is a solution – the medicine of a merry heart.

What is a merry heart? It's the heart which rejoices in something good. This goes back to what we studied earlier. Out of thanksgiving a merry heart is born. Remember our earlier passage, "Be anxious for nothing, but through prayer and supplications with thanksgiving let your request be made known to God?"

The Bible says thanksgiving is our sacrifice that pleases the Lord. We are also told the Lord inhabits the praise of His people. Do you want the Lord to be strong in your life? Offer praise and thanksgiving to Him. Open your eyes and behold the exceedingly precious promises and the benefits He pours into your life.

The Lord promises to show Himself strong on behalf of those whose hearts are completely His.[52] Each morning begin your day by setting your heart upon Him. Think upon His goodness, promises, and blessings. Remember His works and offer thanksgiving for what He has done and is doing. And then yield yourself to His will.

When problems threaten your peace, stop and thank God for what He is doing, for the hope that goes beyond your problems, and ask Him to open your eyes to the eternal perspective of what He's doing in your life. End the day by thanking God for your life, provisions, and promises.

Find a reason to thank the Lord through your problems of the day. This is not to thank God for making you suffer, but for working in the midst of suffering. Then remember to thank Him from the viewpoint of eternity. Will you care about a problem after this life has passed? No. But you will benefit from the refining process if you allow the Lord to do His work.

Be vigilant in thanksgiving[53] and set your emotional table each day. Don't let circumstances set the table for you, or determine the attitudes of your life. Use your positive, God-trusting attitudes to meet the challenges of life and discover the good the Lord has for you in each situation.

Good is there. You must first trust that God has woven good into your life, then adopt a positive attitude by faith, and then by faith seek for His good in every circumstance. You will find it. You will also find the peace of God as He fulfills the promise to guard your heart and mind through Christ.

---

[52] 2 Chronicles 16:9

[53] Colossians 4:2

# Life Applications

- Memorize 1 Thessalonians 5:16-19.
- According to verse 18, what is God's will concerning your attitude?
- Read Psalm 37:4. How do we receive the desires of our heart?
- Think about something that robs you of joy.
  - Plan how you can have an attitude of thanksgiving and delight in God during the tasks which normally sour your attitude.
- Read 1 Corinthians 9:17. Are the tasks of our stewardship optional? What does God reward – the job or the attitude?
- Take time out to set your attitude each morning.
- Take time out to set your attitude before a task you don't enjoy doing.
- Give thanksgiving each day and at least once during the times you feel ungrateful.
- Review Life Applications from previous chapters.

# Dealing with Fear

**John 14:27**

> "Peace I leave with you, My peace I give to you; not as the world gives do I give to you. Let not your heart be troubled, neither let it be afraid. "

Let not your heart be troubled. How many times did Jesus say this and make other similar statements? How can we not fear? Does telling someone not to fear make the fear go away? Of course not. The command to keep our heart from fear and anxiety is not to ignore our emotions or to pretend they don't exist. It's to overcome fear with something greater than fear. Look at **Hebrews 13:6**

> So we may boldly say: "The LORD *is* my helper; I will not fear. What can man do to me?"

Overcoming fear is found through confidence in God. It isn't that fear doesn't exist, but that it loses its grip on our hearts. Fear is not a sin. Fear is not the absence of faith. Fear is of our flesh, but faith is of the Spirit.

As we have already read in scripture, this is the victory that overcomes the world, our faith. Faith in what? Faith in the Lord and His word. And what does the word say? "I give you my peace," therefore, "Do not let your heart be troubled." His peace overcomes our trouble, and the command is to not allow our hearts to displace the peace of God and replace it with the fear that comes through the flesh.

Many great people have been afraid, but faith overcame their fear. When Nehemiah was brokenhearted over the disarray of his homeland, he began to pray for an opportunity to do something. He was a captive from the days when Babylon defeated Israel and was appointed as the cupbearer to King Artaxerxes. He was a slave with no rights. Yet God answered his prayer and the king asked why Nehemiah's expression was sad. In the ancient world, people could be imprisoned or executed for offending the king. Having a bad attitude or a sad expression was considered offensive. That was problem one. Problem two is that he had to give an answer.

How can a slave ask a king to rebuild a city conquered in war? To ask such a thing could be considered treason.

Nehemiah knew this was the opportunity he'd prayed for, but he was about to ask a king to allow him to rebuild a nation once counted as an enemy. It was destroyed in war, and now Nehemiah wanted to ask to rebuild it. That's not something you can ask a pagan king in the ancient world.

Nehemiah gave this testimony, "I became dreadfully afraid." He was treading in dangerous territory, and he knew it. But knowing the Lord was calling him to action, he stepped out in faith. He presented his request and found the king to be receptive. He then took advantage of his opportunity and did something amazing. He asked the king to write letters giving him authority to rebuild, a letter to ask local governors for building materials, and then asked for leave from his duties as the king's servant for an extended period of time.

I would love to have been a fly on the wall and to have witnessed the astonished looks on the faces of those in the king's court. No one asks the king for such favors. Their role was to humor the king and cater to his every whim, yet this slave had the audacity to request something so bold? They probably expected the executioner to be called. Imagine their shock when the king said, "How long will you be gone?"

The man who admitted he was dreadfully afraid did not allow fear to rule him. Instead of trusting in fear, he trusted in the Lord. It's the same heart that King David had several hundred years earlier when he said, "When I'm afraid I will trust in You."

I say 'King David', but he wasn't king when he wrote this. He was running from King Saul, the man who was attempting to thwart God's word by eliminating David so he could preserve the kingdom for his own children. Eventually

David had to flee Israel to escape the army pursuing him, and he ended up in the city of one of his worst enemies.

Remember the story of David and Goliath? Goliath was the champion warrior of the Philistines, and David killed him in a two-man battle. When David fled to Philistia, he was recognized and the army of the Philistines took him to their king. David pretended to be insane so the king wouldn't want him in his presence. While surrounded by enemies, he wrote about his trust in the Lord.

David didn't try to pretend he wasn't afraid. He openly acknowledged his fear, but then put his trust in the Lord. The promises of the Lord sustained David during the darkest moments of his life.

"When I am afraid, I will trust in you." Rather than denying the existence of fear, David dealt with fear in a healthy way. He put his trust in the Lord and refused to allow fear to dominate his heart. He turned from fear by turning to the Lord.

It isn't through denial we overcome fear. Nor is it our human effort that does so. We overcome fear by looking to the Lord and expectantly waiting on His deliverance. Look at **Isaiah 12:2-3**

> 2 Behold, God *is* my salvation, I will trust and not be afraid; 'For YAH, the LORD, *is* my strength and song; He also has become my salvation.' "
> 3 Therefore with joy you will draw water From the wells of salvation.

How is it that we are not afraid? How do we not let our hearts be troubled? By turning our hearts to trust in God's deliverance so our focus is no longer on the trouble that makes us afraid. Salvation doesn't only mean the salvation of our souls that brings us into the faith. As is in the passage above, salvation also means to be saved from something threatening us.

Why will I not be afraid? Because the Lord becomes my strength. It isn't merely an attempt to hide from fear, but it is turning from fear and toward the Lord. It is His power and He delivers those who trust in Him.

Faith calls us to believe that God is in control, not circumstances. Do you remember when the disciples were caught in a severe storm? The ship was taking on water and in desperation, they woke Jesus from sleep and said, "Do you not care that we are perishing?"[54]

Jesus arose and rebuked the storms. While they stood amazed at His power, Jesus said, "Why are you so fearful? How is it that you have no faith?"

Faith in what? They were called by Christ for the purpose of completing the work of God. God watches over the sparrows, and since He declared that we are more valuable than sparrows, it is obvious He watches over us. Did the disciples think that Jesus' plan would be drowned in the storm? That isn't possible. Nothing can thwart the plan of God, and those walking in His calling cannot perish until the Lord calls them home.

Their failure was not in waking Jesus and asking for help. The failure was that they panicked in the storm and lashed out at God. "Do you not care that I am perishing," is not a prayer of faith. Prayer should be to express our trust that God will either calm the storm, or guide us through it. It is to be confident that no power in heaven or earth can stand against the will of God, or against us fulfilling His will.

Let me give one more example before we move on. Jacob fled his home to live with an uncle because his brother Esau had vowed to kill him for taking the family inheritance. After several years with his uncle, the Lord commanded Jacob to return home with the promise that God would be with him.

Knowing his brother might be still angry, he sent messengers to greet his brother. The messengers returned with bad news. "Your brother is coming and has gathered

---

[54] Mark 4:38

four-hundred men." That wasn't good. Clearly the intent was to slaughter Jacob and anyone who might be with him. The natural response would be to turn around and flee, but look at Jacob's prayer in **Genesis 32:9-12**

9 Then Jacob said, "O God of my father Abraham and God of my father Isaac, the LORD who said to me, 'Return to your country and to your family, and I will deal well with you':

10 "I am not worthy of the least of all the mercies and of all the truth which You have shown Your servant; for I crossed over this Jordan with my staff, and now I have become two companies.

11 "Deliver me, I pray, from the hand of my brother, from the hand of Esau; for I fear him, lest he come and attack me *and* the mother with the children.

12 "For You said, 'I will surely treat you well, and make your descendants as the sand of the sea, which cannot be numbered for multitude.' "

Jacob didn't put himself in harm's way. He followed God into harm's way. The two companies refers to his family. He divided his children and wives (for multiple wives were common in that era) into two groups and separated them. The hope was that if Esau attacked one, the rest of the family could escape.

Notice Jacob's prayer. "I fear him (Esau)." He didn't deny his fears. Nor did he allow fear to turn his heart back. If he had been driven away by fear, he would have never seen the promises of God. Instead, Jacob put his faith in the word of the Lord and put his trust in God. He stood upon the promise in spite of his fear.

How encouraging this should be for us. In the midst of an amazing prayer of faith, Jacob acknowledges his fear. Fear didn't overcome faith; faith overcame fear. This is the message of faith. When Jesus said to not be anxious, not to be afraid, and to not allow our hearts to be troubled, this is what He is talking about.

Anxiety rises up and tries to rule our hearts, but we don't allow anxiety to take over and trouble our lives. Fear troubles our hearts and attempts to make us flee, but we stand upon our faith in the Lord and allow Him to overcome the things that cause fear. Fear is the flesh rising up to take over our minds, but we are called to cast it down through the Spirit and take each thought captive to the obedience of Christ.

What if our fear is the result of something beyond our control? The Lord is the master of the storms, and nothing is beyond His control. In fact, the Bible teaches that everything in the universe is held together by the word of His power. If this is true (and it is), then the circumstances that threaten us can only exist within His control. God has the power over trouble – not the other way around.

What if my fear is irrational? Sometimes we are afraid without a clear cause. Again, everything is subject to the Lord. He will allow our lives to be tested, but no one who stands upon faith can be overcome. Don't lose sight of our original passage from **2 Timothy 1:7**

For God has not given us a spirit of fear, but of power and of love and of a sound mind.

The spirit of fear is not from God; therefore, it can only have one source. The Bible says Satan roams about seeking whom he may destroy. He provokes us through the flesh and will provoke others against us. Yet the scripture also says the devil has no power over those who abide in God's presence. Jesus referred to Satan as a thief who seeks to steal, kill, and destroy. Yet we have something greater. **1 John 4:4**

You are of God, little children, and have overcome them, because He who is in you is greater than he who is in the world.

Consider the power of this promise. It follows the passage which warns about the spirit of the antichrist that has gone into the world. Antichrist doesn't only refer to the man of sin we see in the book of Revelation, but it also refers to the spirit of deception that emanates from the devil. This false spirit (the same one that creates the spirit of fear) has gone into the world for the purpose of creating confusion, robbing people of peace, and driving people away from the will of God.

In spite of all this, we have an amazing promise. Because we are of God through Christ, we have overcome them. Who have we overcome? Any spirit, any deception, anything that is of the world. The reason – greater is He who is in you than he who is in the world. The Spirit of God within you is greater than anything of the world. That includes fear, sin, enemies, disease, or any other thing which attempts to overcome the believer. God is greater. He has no rivals. Satan is not a rival god; He is a spirit and is subject to the word of God just like everything else in this universe. He too is dependent upon God for life and existence.

The problem with the flesh is it is easily manipulated. This is why we are promised if we walk in the Spirit, the flesh has no power over us. God is Spirit. Through His Spirit we have life. Jesus said in order to be a worshiper of God we must be in Spirit and truth. When we walk in the Spirit, fear cannot remain. It will call and attempt to manipulate you, but the body of sin has been done away with. Since the spirit of fear is dependent upon attacking you through the flesh, it has no power over you, unless you submit yourself to it.

The more we live in fear, the more fear takes root in our minds. Living in fear eventually changes our patterns of thinking and we will begin to allow negative emotions to rule our minds. The more our minds are made subject to negative patterns of thinking, the more we allow them to rule.

There is one truth few Christians live by. Though our problems may be rooted in the physical, these do not have the power to overcome the Spirit of God within us. When we walk in the Spirit, the flesh has no power over us. That includes our physical minds. If you are in Christ, you have the power to rise above the demands of the flesh. This is true even if they are physical in nature.

Physical addictions are broken through the Spirit of God. This does not mean they are easily broken, for our entire pattern of behavior is now habitually in the flesh. I can say this from personal experience. Because we are conditioned to think and act through the flesh, we are naturally drawn by the flesh, even when we know the action is harmful. It may seem like the flesh has an unbreakable grip, but it doesn't. That's part of the deception. As long as we are intimidated into submission, our flesh continues to rule, but the promise we have is, "If you walk in the Spirit, you shall not fulfill the lusts of the flesh."[55]

As a child I was exposed to things that completely shaped my mind. During those development years, these patterns of thinking were so engrained into my life I didn't believe it was possible to overcome. Even as a Christian, I was not able to overcome. I won't give specifics because it equally applies to many areas of life and struggles we go through. Think upon your personal struggles. That was where I stood. And it ruled me for most of my life.

There is something about exposure to harmful behaviors as a child that programs the brain for adulthood. Whether it be brooding, anger, lust, dwelling on sorrow, self-centeredness, or any number of other behaviors, the mind is developed early on. The same is true for positive ways. Children who are encouraged, loved, and taught to develop healthy attitudes tend to be better adjusted. However, sometimes a child can be stubborn and refuse good counsel.

Even in a healthy environment, people can develop harmful ways of thinking. Such was I. Through my own

---

[55] Galatians 5:16

choices, I laid a poor foundation which created mountains to overcome later in life.

The mind in early years is shaped for lifelong processes. This is why kids exposed to music early have a tendency to become musically inclined. Or kids exposed to the outdoors grow up loving the outdoors. This is also true for athletics, academics, and many other areas of life. There are exceptions, but the truth is we develop bents toward areas we practice early in life. This is also why abused children have lifelong struggles and deep-rooted emotional problems.

Fast forward a few decades and what happens? Learning new things is more challenging and deprogramming destructive behaviors and ways of thinking become more difficult. We can't say, "Stop thinking that way," and expect a change. Scars run deep and often the brain is developed in ways that are difficult to reprogram. People who grow up in fear, regardless of the cause, have a bent toward fear. This is true even when there doesn't seem to be a rational reason.

I'm using fear as the main topic, but these things we are discussing apply to any pattern of thinking that is destructive.

Overcoming these things is hard to put into words, for there isn't a step-by-step instruction. The Lord has to open our eyes and enlighten our understanding. Deliverance comes from His Spirit within us, not by our outward practices. Though deliverance is of the Spirit, there are also practical things we must do.

Let me explain. Applying ourselves to spiritual disciplines is not what changes our lives. God transforms us by His Spirit, and renews our minds with the Word. However, there must be disciplines in our lives in order for us to understand spiritual principles and learn what it means to truly seek the Lord. I can't walk in the Spirit if I don't know what the Bible teaches about it. Yet, knowing the Bible alone isn't enough. I learn, and then I cry out to the Lord for wisdom, understanding, and knowledge of Him and His ways.

I had studied the word for years, but I still struggled with areas of my life I couldn't control. I would have short victories, but the old patterns of thinking would rise up again and take over my mind. Yet one day things changed. I had a major breakthrough when I read a passage I had gone through dozens of times. I spoke about this in an earlier chapter, but it's important enough to go over again. If you grasp the magnitude of this passage, it's probably the single most important thing after understanding grace. Take this passage to heart, **Romans 6:6-7**

6 Knowing this, that our old man was crucified with *Him*, that the body of sin might be done away with, that we should no longer be slaves of sin.

7 For he who has died has been freed from sin.

If you are born again, your old man (old nature and old ways of thinking) have been crucified with Christ. It *has been* done away with. Not 'will be', but 'has been'. It's dead. In Christ you died. That is what salvation is all about. Your old life was surrendered to God for the purpose of crucifying your flesh (old sinful nature) so you could be raised as a new creation. The body of sin has been done away with. You are no longer its slave.

Depression enslaves our minds. Fear enslaves our minds. Lust enslaves our minds. Greed enslaves our minds. Anything that puts our minds under its control is part of the old life. It has been done away with and God has promised that I am no longer under its control. Let this sink in and take it to heart. You are no longer under its control.

While this is true, we also know through the teachings found in Romans 7, the sin in our flesh will rise up and try to bring our minds back into slavery. This can only happen if you submit to it. You submit to it by agreeing to follow it back into bondage.

Lust lures us with empty promises. It deceives us into following it back into the old lifestyle. When we do, it will take over our minds and attempt to keep us from escaping.

Anger, fear, and depression are the same way. They will rise up and attempt to war against your mind. If you try to resist, it will increase the battle and demand submission. It's like a bully that intimidates his victim into submission.

When I was about six, a friend of mine was being chased by a bully on the playground. The kid was big and he looked tough. As my friend ran in circles around the monkey bars, he kept crying out, "Help me, Eddie." I didn't want to fight this bully because he would have slaughtered me. But about the fifth time my friend begged for my help, I jumped down.

I was a skinny kid, and a bit nerdy. I had never seen the bully before, and he had never seen me. This played to my advantage. I stepped between my friend and the bully and he stopped. He gave me an evil stare, and I stared back. He tried to step around me, but I stepped in front of him again. He stepped to the left, and I stepped in front of him. He stepped to the right, and I did it again. After a few more waltzes, he stared at me for a long moment, then turned and walked away. I was very relieved. Apparently he wanted a victim who didn't pose a threat.

This is the flesh. It has no power, for all we must do is turn and call to Christ. Unlike my skinny little self, He has the power to crucify the flesh. But this only happens when we look to the cross and place our trust in Him. Until then, it bullies us into submission and defeats us – not because it has power over us, but because we submit to it. Instead of turning to Christ for help, we run in circles or cower in fear. Or we obey its demands. Yet when we realize the bully has no power, things change. Our human effort can't defeat the flesh, but we can step into the Spirit where it has no ability to threaten us.

The amazing passage in Romans 6 above changed my life. In the past, my flesh demanded submission. I tried to resist, but it chased me down. It then demanded my obedience and I felt powerless to resist. I then became its slave again.

Something amazing happened when I read the promise that the flesh no longer has dominion over me, for it has been crucified. Then I found Romans 6:13-14. Here I am promised sin cannot have dominion over me unless I present myself to it as a slave. Unless I turn toward the sin, it cannot take over my mind. Instead, I must turn to the cross and declare my faith in the promise, "I have been crucified with Christ. He has done away with the old nature so it no longer has dominion over me." I believe God, and He steps in to fulfill His promise.

It's so simple, yet I never grasped this truth until my eyes were opened. Perhaps this needs to be your prayer – to ask God to open your eyes.

When fear comes calling, it no longer has dominion over you. It wars against you through the flesh, but it's a meaningless attack if you are walking in the Spirit by looking to the cross and walking with the Lord. He rescues us from the power of the flesh.

It's not that the flesh has changed. It still has the same weaknesses and sinful passions, but it loses dominion over us. It may demand our allegiance through various temptations, but look to the cross, where your deliverance has already been purchased. As you learn what it means to walk consistently in the Spirit, the temptation to return to the flesh loses its grip. It still calls, but you'll learn to refuse its demands.

This is true for every Christian. It's not easy to ignore the flesh. In fact, through your own effort, it's impossible to resist. But you have the God given power to walk in the Spirit and not be ruled by the flesh. Do you believe?

Just as you trusted in Christ for salvation, so you must trust in Christ to overcome. We are saved from our sins without any effort on our part. We look to the cross, believe in what Jesus did for us, and release our lives into His trust.

God then intervenes to take our old sinful ways, place a new spirit within us, and we become a new creation. We are now born anew. We did nothing to earn our new life and we certainly did nothing to create the new life within us. We believed, put our trust in Christ, and He stepped in to do the work.

Nothing changes after salvation. The Christian life is lived the same way we received this new life. We see His word, believe, and put our trust in Him. God then intervenes to empower us to live and walk in the Spirit. The flesh tries to draw our attention to the things of the flesh, but God calls us to turn to Him, believe, and walk in the Spirit. It is God who steps in when we turn to Him by faith. It is His work.

Rather than you overcoming the flesh by your efforts, you are transformed into an overcomer by the power of Christ. Believe and receive. That is the message of the gospel. It's the message of God's call to come to Christ, and it's also God's call to live and abide in Christ so you can fulfill the Christian walk of victory.

Live in your transformed life.

# Life Applications

- Memorize Psalm 56:3-4
- Identify the types of things in life that cause you to feel anxious. List them in a journal.
- Search for scriptures that address these issues. Here are some examples:
  - Matthew 6:25-33 - God provides food, water, and clothing.
  - Psalm 31:19-20 - God protects from the plotting of man.
  - Psalm 27:3-6 - God's protection during war.
  - Psalm 91:4-7 - God's protection from disasters.
  - Psalm 79:9 - God delivers us from our sins.
- Pray for God to open your eyes to walk in the Spirit.
- Pray to the Lord declaring your trust in the promises of His word while setting your heart on obedience to His commands.
- Review Life Applications from previous chapters.

# Take Every Thought Captive

**2 Corinthians 10:4-6**

> 4 For the weapons of our warfare *are* not carnal but mighty in God for pulling down strongholds, 5 casting down arguments and every high thing that exalts itself against the knowledge of God, bringing every thought into captivity to the obedience of Christ, 6 and being ready to punish all disobedience when your obedience is fulfilled.

In a previous chapter we laid the foundation this section will build upon. Since so much of our life is affected by our thought life, it's necessary to break the topic into smaller bites. Now that we've explored how we view problems, set our emotional table, and pray with diligence, it's time to go a little deeper into the process of controlling our thought life in a healthy way.

Controlling thoughts is a difficult process. For some, it can seem like a nearly impossible goal. Don't be discouraged. Everyone struggles to control his or her thought life to some degree. When we're angry, what do we do? We allow bitter thoughts to race through our heads as we relive the offense, analyze it, and often think on how we would like to make it right based on our own standard of justice.

People who are susceptible to sensuality often struggle with lustful thoughts, imaginations, and they harbor impure ideas in their hearts. Others can't let go of wrongs, and fill their time brooding over the injustices they have experienced. Some cling to heartaches, insecurities, and any number of harmful imaginations. Each person struggles with some type of mental battle, but there is a way of escape.

If we allow our thoughts to rule, we are surrendering our minds to the flesh, and eventually these things will come out in our life and conversations. In a recent news story a man who lost his job eighteen months ago returned to his old company to murder his former boss. This means for a year and a half, this man brooded over his anger until it consumed him. Many lives were destroyed, beginning with the brooder, because the truth of scripture was ignored. God has given us a way of escape, but each of us must be willing to apply the Lord's instructions.

Whether our minds are focusing upon sensuality, fear, greed, bitterness, revenge, self-pity, or any other thing, our thoughts can become obsessive and destructive.

Some are obsessive about worry. Others obsess over money. Some are consumed with thoughts about vengeance. We've all heard stories about people snapping, but what precedes this? People who snap into violence frequently have expressed an unhealthy focus on wrongs being done to them. Others become overwhelmed with the evils of society. Sometimes the snapping is internally focused as people think suicidal thoughts or deface themselves. Others simply lose their ability to cope and snap into a nervous breakdown.

Each of these has one thing in common. They become obsessed in a pattern of thought and lose control of the ability to direct their focus to healthy habits and ways of thinking.

While it may sound odd, even religious obsessions can be destructive. People who love the Bible and want to please God can lose control and turn Christianity into a style of religion that is dependent upon their efforts. They begin beating themselves up for every negative thought and try to overcome by flooding their lives with religious practices and spiritual babblings.

I say babblings not because the words are not coherent, but because the words have become their addiction rather than an expression of their trust in the Lord. Speaking religious things will not transform our lives or change our circumstances, for as the Bible says, the Kingdom of God is not in word, but in God's power.[56]

A common practice I've seen among Christians is to rebuke Satan each time they feel tempted or have an unexpected thought. There are two problems with this. First, it doesn't work. People who make a habit of rebuking the devil have no better success in living holy lives than those who don't. Oftentimes they have less success because their focus is off target. Second, the Bible never instructs us to speak to the devil. Not one time do we see anyone in scripture rebuking Satan for the problems in their life. Not one of the apostles practiced this, nor did they teach it to others.

When the Apostle Paul lamented about the sin warring against his mind, he didn't blame the devil, he blamed his flesh. It was sin dwelling in his flesh that attempted to rise up, draw his mind out of the Spirit and into the flesh, and bring him back under bondage to sin. It is true that the devil is our tempter, but he does so by appealing to the desires of our flesh.

When we are looking for someone else to blame – including the devil – we are not focusing on the root of the problem. The root of the problem is within us, that is in our flesh. Until we recognize our personal responsibility, we will never effectively get our lives under control. Things outside of ourselves may indeed tempt us, but the heart of the problem is our own desires. And when we are tempted, we need to turn (repent).

Repentance is not to scorn ourselves or to grovel in a self-debasing attitude. Repentance is to recognize something we are doing is wrong, and then turning from that and toward the right way. Repentance for the unbeliever is to recognize they are going in the opposite direction and to turn from their own ways and toward God. Repentance in the life of a believer is to recognize we are drifting off course,

---

[56] 1 Corinthians 4:20

and do a course correction. It could be a slight correction, or a major one. But one thing we must keep in mind is the problem of temptation comes from within our own flesh.

It's interesting that in the book of James in the Bible, the church is rebuked for the idea some people had. They were teaching that God tempts us with sin. James corrects this erroneous way of thinking, but he never mentions the devil. Instead he says, "We are tempted when we are drawn by our own lusts and enticed." The source of temptation is within your flesh. Satan is doing nothing but presenting the things you already want. The solution is not to rebuke the devil, but to turn from and depart from temptation, and deny the flesh.

We are given the promise of self-control, but it isn't through human effort. Self-control is a fruit of the Spirit. (See Galatians 5:22-25). In Galatians, the fruit of the Spirit is presented after the works of the flesh have been identified. The Bible lists the works of the flesh – things that tempt us, destroy us, create ungodly behaviors, etc. Then the Bible presents the solution – the fruit of the Spirit. In fact, before listing the works of the flesh, the Bible promises, "Walk in the Spirit and you will not fulfill the lusts of the flesh." Then the explanation is given to contrast sinful works against spiritual fruit. To make sure we understand, we are told these two, the flesh and the Spirit, are at war and can never agree.

This takes us right back to our passage at the beginning of this chapter. It begins with the statement, "The weapons of our warfare are not carnal (physical), but spiritual."

If you attempt to win your mind by human effort, you are already on the losing side. It's a war between the flesh, where Satan has the dominion, and the Spirit, where God reigns. To think you can fight Satan with your own words is to use human effort to fight against human nature. Both are of the flesh and the flesh cannot produce spiritual fruit. Only God can produce fruit in our lives.

Self-control is the fruit of the Spirit. It is founded upon the love of God that has already been poured into our hearts (See Romans 5:5). When we are walking in the Spirit, spiritual fruit will begin emerging from our lives. This includes self-control. Controlling our thoughts is part of self-control. When the flesh is how we make our stand and how we try to live out our faith, it's a guaranteed failure. At best, it is worthless fruit. We cannot produce the fruit of the Spirit, but instead we'll see works of the flesh appearing in our lives.

Though we might have limited success battling the things that are not major character flaws, we still cannot produce righteousness in our lives based on what we don't do. Nor can we produce righteousness based on what we do. God produces spiritual things, we produce physical things. To experience God's peace, love, joy, goodness, patience, faith, gentleness, and self-control, we must be walking in the Spirit.

The spiritual attacks against you serve no other purpose than to get you into the flesh where you are no longer standing upon the strength of the Lord and the power of His might.[57]

Many battles are fought in the mind. To be carnally minded is death, but to be spiritually minded is life and peace. (Romans 8:6) Or as the Apostle Paul also stated, "With my mind I serve the law of God, but with the flesh, the law of sin."

Let's look at thoughts for a moment. As stated before, not every thought which pops in your head is yours. Strange thoughts may indeed pop into your mind. It could be thoughts of lust, greed, hatred, or any other ungodly thing. A thought is not yours until you accept and receive it into your heart. Every thought is an offering, but you do not have to receive every offer given.

---

[57] Ephesians 6:10

Take Every Thought Captive

The truth is that Satan knows your weaknesses. He knows what you react to. And he will continue to feed to you what is working. The answer is not to rebuke Satan. He cares nothing about your words. However, He does care about whether you are in the Spirit. He cannot go where you and the Lord abide, but he can draw you to where he abides.

Rebuking Satan doesn't stop the thoughts. If anything, it creates a new obsession, where you are now depending on yourself rather than the Spirit of God. Here is the power of resisting Satan, as described in the Bible. Look again at **James 4:6-8**

6 But He gives more grace. Therefore He says: "God resists the proud, But gives grace to the humble."

7 Therefore submit to God. Resist the devil and he will flee from you.

8 Draw near to God and He will draw near to you. Cleanse *your* hands, *you* sinners; and purify *your* hearts, *you* double-minded.

Does this passage tell us if we resist the devil he flees? No it doesn't. People often misunderstand this. This passage says, "Submit to God," and then "Resist the devil." Without submission to God, there is no power in resistance. The resistance is you resisting the devil's luring of your desires.

If you are in the Spirit, the devil attempts to draw you into the flesh. But you must resist and continue to abide with the Lord. You resist by looking to the cross where your deliverance was purchased. On the cross we find the power of Christ to strengthen us, and we also find the place of crucifixion, where our flesh is put to death. We look to Jesus, the Author and Finisher of our faith, and He draws us near as we let go of the flesh and draw near to Him. We put our trust in His power and the flesh is put to death again, and in Christ our spirit is renewed with His power and life.

When you take heed to God's call to draw near to Him, He has promised to draw near to you. It is God drawing you into the Spirit – a place the devil cannot go. That coward flees from God, so when you are submitting to God, the devil has no choice but to flee.

To make resistance your strength is to make the flesh your strength. This is a far cry from the victory that overcomes the world – our faith.

So what happens when a bad thought enters your mind? It's simple. Reject it. It's not yours, so why should you fret over it. This was Satan's offering and you simply decline and turn away from it. If it returns, reject it again. It is not yours. You are not accountable for it. And you will not be judged for it. Even if it's the most blasphemous thought a human has ever conceived, it doesn't matter. It's not yours unless you accept it and cultivate the thought in your heart.

Let's dig into this further by looking at the words of Jesus found in **Mark 7:18-23**

18 So He said to them, "Are you thus without understanding also? Do you not perceive that whatever enters a man from outside cannot defile him,

19 "because it does not enter his heart but his stomach, and is eliminated, *thus* purifying all foods?"

20 And He said, "What comes out of a man, that defiles a man.

21 "For from within, out of the heart of men, proceed evil thoughts, adulteries, fornications, murders,

22 "thefts, covetousness, wickedness, deceit, lewdness, an evil eye, blasphemy, pride, foolishness.

23 "All these evil things come from within and defile a man."

What a freeing passage! Though the subject is food, it doesn't only apply to food. What goes into man cannot defile him. It's what comes out that defiles him. Why? Because what comes out of your mouth and comes out in your behaviors are the things you have accepted into your heart by welcoming them into your mind.

If you watch television shows that are immoral, what is happening? You are welcoming those things into your mind, which opens the door to your heart. The Bible warns us to guard our hearts with all diligence, for out of the heart come the issues of life.[58] How do you guard your heart? Your mind is your gatekeeper. What you accept in your mind you are giving access to your heart. That is true whether it be TV, movies, music, sinful actions, or thoughts. Until you receive it into your heart, it cannot produce sin. Out of the heart proceeds evil. Consider **Luke 6:45**

A good man out of the good treasure of his heart brings forth good; and an evil man out of the evil treasure of his heart brings forth evil. For out of the abundance of the heart his mouth speaks.

Who is the good man? Good comes from God alone; therefore, the good man is the person who is abiding in Christ and receiving the goodness of God.

The message is clear. Each thing you accept becomes something you treasure. If you treasure sin, you will store sin in your heart. And then it will come out in your life. Unfortunately, we all have a bent toward sin and naturally want to store up the things we lust after. However, as we discover the true treasures of God's word, we begin to store His word in our heart and receive the promise that this is how we cleanse our ways. "Your word have I hidden in my heart that I might not sin against You."[59]

What you treasure is what you will produce.

So when a thought arises, it isn't yours until you value it enough to receive it. If you want to be angry, you will treasure anger in your heart and produce bitterness in your life. If you want to have self-pity, you will treasure those thoughts, dwell on them, cultivate them, and they will emerge from your heart and into your life to produce

---

[58] Proverbs 4:23
[59] Psalm 119:9-11

destructive behaviors, negative conversations, and damaging emotions. This is true for every form of habitual sin.

Thoughts have no power over you until you receive them. The problem isn't Satan. He will always be the tempter. Those who receive his offerings will reap the fruit of sin and be driven by their desires. However, those who refuse his offerings will see them lose their power.

What will happen is that you'll attempt to resist, but the thoughts will keep coming. The enemy's goal is to wear you down, or catch you in a moment of vulnerability or weakness.

We are not only resisting, but turning toward the Lord. Our minds cannot operate in a vacuum. An empty mind is vulnerable to anything. Instead we are called to engage our minds by thinking on these things.

Remember our passages from Philippians 4? Whatever things are lovely, whatever things are good, whatever things are pure, of good report, etc. Think on these things. And then believe the promise that the God of peace will guard your hearts and minds through Christ. This is the call of faith. It's a call to leave the fleshly mind behind and take on the spiritual mind where there is life and peace.

It won't be easy. We have a lifetime of habits and programming of our thoughts to overcome. It's for this reason we have the scriptures to guide us. Let's review our introductory passage for this chapter again so we can glean from its truth. **2 Corinthians 10:4-6**

4 For the weapons of our warfare *are* not carnal but mighty in God for pulling down strongholds,

5 casting down arguments and every high thing that exalts itself against the knowledge of God, bringing every thought into captivity to the obedience of Christ,

6 and being ready to punish all disobedience when your obedience is fulfilled.

Negative thinking becomes a stronghold. A stronghold is a place in enemy territory where an opponent has gotten an advantage. They have taken ground, entrenched themselves, and now have a strategic advantage to launch a campaign to take more ground. This is the fleshly mind. It could even be your mind right now. Yet notice how the Bible addresses it. You have the power to pull down that stronghold, but not by human effort. Your weapon is not of the flesh, but of the Spirit. It's the power of God given to you through God's Spirit and His word.

We've already discussed how this applies to thoughts, but it also applies to rooting out negative patterns of thinking. These thoughts exalt themselves against the knowledge of God. Therefore, you and I are called to take God's mighty weapon and cast down that offender.

The weapon is the word of God and faith. According to the scriptures, the word of God is our sword of the Spirit and faith is the victory that overcomes the world. This includes the thoughts born of the world that attempt to invade our minds. Or ways of thinking that have already established strongholds in our minds.

The first thing in any war is to cut off the supply line. Don't feed your mind the things you are trying to root out of your life. Don't watch shows that create temptation or teach things that oppose obedience to Christ. Don't allow your mind to dwell on the things you are trying to extract. You may even have to sever destructive relationships. Consider **Proverbs 22:24-25**

24 Make no friendship with an angry man, And with a furious man do not go,

25 Lest you learn his ways And set a snare for your soul.

The same principle would apply to any relationship where the person is a bad influence. I worked with a man who was always negative. I liked him and for a time we hung out together, but I eventually realized the negative influence he was having on me. He talked about everything as if it were doom and gloom. The company was heading to bankruptcy, the country was going to hell in a hand-basket, people were doing things we needed to be concerned about. After spending a few hours together, I felt depressed and hopeless. I finally realized I didn't need to hang around this person. Since I could not influence him, I determined not to allow his negativism to influence me.

We all come across people like this. There is even a so-called Christian discernment site I used to visit. A while back I realized it was nothing but a gossip site. It was a place where any perceived flaw or mistake was exploited and made into a public spectacle. Under the pretense of exposing errors in the church, this site turned people's hearts against their brethren and gave a negative view on nearly every aspect of the church.

Christian discernments, conspiracy theories, politics, and gossip can all play roles in creating negative attitudes that hinder our faith. While it may seem entertaining to hear these things, the truth is it's not of God. The litmus test is not to say, "Well, there's nothing wrong with it." The test is, does it glorify Christ? Does it create the right spirit within us?

There are times when real problems need to be addressed. Get informed with the facts, resolve the problem, and get out. Don't live among the naysayers. If something cannot be changed, it's not for us to wallow in the failure of others. Nor is it good to wallow in our own failures.

Don't surround yourself with people, books, shows, music, or anything else that can add a snare to your soul. When you must be around someone like that, take time out to renew your mind and return to the joy of the Lord.

We are commanded to take every thought captive. This means you are appointed by the Lord to police your thoughts. When something comes in, you have the authority by God to take it captive and expel it.

Sometimes your mind will drift and it's not until you feel your emotions rising that you realize you are dwelling on something that opposes the commandment of God to be spiritually minded. Don't turn this slip into a big deal. Once you recognize it, rise up in obedience, take it captive, and evict it from your mind. If it returns, take it captive again. And again. And as many times as it is necessary. At first it will seem like thoughts are swarming like bees, but in time they will begin to lose their tenacity and the victory is yours.

One thing about thoughts; they are either your enemies or allies. And you must determine which side you are on. If you join the enemy, then you make yourself into an ally for the flesh in its war against the Spirit. There are no passive observers. A guard who rejects his duty is an ally of the invader.

Let's examine the last major point of our main passage. Once you fulfill the command to take every thought captive, there is one final instruction – be ready to avenge all disobedience once your obedience is fulfilled.

Don't get these two out of order. Until you master your thought life through submission to the Spirit, you cannot avenge anything. If my thoughts are the problem, how can I correct anything else? I must first receive the promise of a sound mind before I can think clearly enough to discern what obedience is, much less how to avenge disobedience.

Finally, we need to understand what it means to avenge disobedience. This is not you avenging wrongs. The Bible has already addressed this concern when God said, "Do not avenge yourselves – vengeance is mine, says the Lord." The vengeance of disobedience is to correct what is wrong – beginning with yourself and then becoming a light to the world.

To understand this more fully, let's look at the Greek word translated into avenge. It's the word 'ekdikeo', which means:

> To avenge, make right, do justice to something or someone.

It does not mean to retaliate. It means to make what is unjust become just. It means to take something that is wrong and correct it. That begins first with our lives. It's the same as we examined from Jesus' command to remove the plank from our own eye before attempting to help remove the speck from our brother's eye.

There are many wrongs in the world. When we see an injustice, we want to do something about it. However, if we are far from the justice of God, we will lack the discernment to determine what is right or how to correct it. This is what leads misguided people to kill in the name of God. Or to war against others in the church. We see an offense and we may want to do good, but if we are warring according to the flesh, we become the problem. Even if we're well-intentioned, if we're in the flesh we are part of the world and are propagating the problem.

Our weapons are not physical. We first pursue obedience and take every thought captive to the obedience of Christ. We then cast down strongholds in our lives as we learn what it means to walk in the Spirit. Then we avenge the disobedience of our own lives so we are unhindered in our obedience, and then we can be instruments of change in the lives of others. And we do so by taking them down the same path we are walking – not brow-beating them into submission. We must become leaders by example, not enforcers.

Another important truth about avenging disobedience is how it applies to self-examination. I may recognize many faults in my own life. These things hammer at my self-confidence and sense of self-worth. When I see my deep-rooted character flaws, I am not called to beat myself up over them. Nor am I called to tackle them right away. The root of the problem must be fixed first, before I can fix anything else.

If my thought life is out of control, I don't need to overwhelm myself by trying to control other behaviors by mere human effort. How can I fix my behavior when my flesh is ruling my mind? I can't.

This is why the Bible presents this truth as it is written. If I can stop doing something easily, by all means I should stop the destructive behavior. However, if it is something that dominates my life, though it may be disobedient to Christ, it isn't my first concern. My first concern is to take back the stronghold of my mind, and then I will be in a position to avenge my destructive behaviors.

I first learn what it means to take every thought captive. Once my obedience in this area is fulfilled, I can then avenge the disobedience of the flesh in other areas of my life. Many times, the destructive behavior is corrected once our thoughts are correct.

Some people are addicted to gambling. Try as they might, the gambling frequently gets the upper hand. The truth is that gambling is not the problem. It's a symptom of the problem. The problem is their way of thinking which leads to the desire expressed through gambling. At the heart is a love of money. When that way of thinking is corrected, the desire to gain more will also dissipate. But if someone tackles the addiction without changing their way of thinking, the best they can hope for is a temporary fix.

People spend their lives gaining ground against their addiction only to lose it when their minds return to their desire. If the mind is already pursuing a desire, our behavior will soon follow.

This can be true for any addiction or destructive behavior. The addiction and behavior is the symptom. The problem of taking back our thoughts and guarding our hearts must first be accomplished before the behavior can be avenged.

Let me reiterate this important point. Once our minds are sober and we are thinking soundly, we then control the stronghold and have the power to avenge disobedience in our own lives.

The truth is that every person has this problem. The symptoms may be different, and some expressions of our desires are socially acceptable. Maybe even praised. A workaholic is a struggling person, but since his excessive work produces wealth, it is considered an achievement. But what is achieved? Nothing of eternal value. They are achieving something temporary by sacrificing relationships and abandoning the calling of God. In the end, they will have gained nothing eternal for a lifetime of labor.

Each person battles their thought life in different ways. Only when outward behavior is clearly harmful does anyone recognize the danger. Yet these principles apply to us all. Each person must learn to identify thoughts, take them captive, and battle through this life in obedience to the Holy Spirit in order to find true peace and victory.

God has given these instructions for a reason. The struggles are real, and anyone who fails to recognize their need is forfeiting the true treasure of knowing God. What's more, every single person has the victory already given.

Everyone has the promise that the Lord is their strength. Our battle is to depart from the flesh and abide in the Spirit. It's all about walking with God in intimate fellowship.

To be spiritually minded is life and peace.[60] This is where the joy of the Christian life begins. Take every thought captive – walk in the Spirit, experience the fullness of Christ. It's yours if you believe God, apply His truth, and walk in these principles.

---

[60] Romans 8:6

# Life Applications

- Memorize 2 Corinthians 10:4-5
- Think about the things that influence your mind - TV, Music, Books, Internet, etc.
- Identify the things which have a negative influence and replace them with godly activities.
- Read James 4:6-8.
- Why does James begin this instruction by telling us God resists the proud but gives grace to the Humble?
- If we refuse to submit something to God, is this an act of pride?
- Think about thoughts and habits that seem to have a stronghold on you. Submit yourself to God as you turn your heart away from ungodly thoughts or activities.
- Take time to review Life Applications from previous chapters.

# Restoring Relationships

**Proverbs 18:19**

>A brother offended *is harder to win* than a strong city,
>And contentions *are* like the bars of a castle.

Conflict is a part of life. It's how we handle conflict that impacts our relationships. We offend others just as often as we are offended, but we only notice what affects our personal feelings. The scriptures instruct us not to be an offense to anyone, but as with most commands, we will fall short more times than we'd like to admit.

When it comes to offenses, our responsibility is twofold. We are called to reconcile and we are called to forgive. Consider the words of Jesus in **Matthew 5:23-24**

>23 Therefore if you bring your gift to the altar, and there remember your brother has something against you,
>24 leave your gift there before the altar, and go your way. First be reconciled to your brother, and then come and offer your gift.

Notice the focus of this passage. We are the offender. When we are seeking the Lord, He will often remind us of these offenses and embittered relationships, then call us to reconcile. Not every person will forgive, but it is our responsibility to seek reconciliation. And we do so by taking ownership of the offense and doing what is in our power to make it right. It shouldn't be difficult, but human nature has a hard time accepting personal faults.

When we are the offended party, the Bible gives us clear instructions on this as well. Look at **Matthew 18:15**

>15 Moreover if your brother sins against you, go and tell him his fault between you and him alone. If he hears you, you have gained your brother.

The passages we are discussing mention brothers, but the principle is for all. This scripture goes on to discuss how to respond if your brother doesn't reconcile, but I won't get into this here. The point is that instead of seeking reconciliation, we have the tendency of harboring secret bitterness.

People will be offended and angry with us, but we won't even know why. We sever relationships with others, and they never know why. The truth most offenses are unintentional and could easily be reconciled, but we don't follow God's design for restoration. Instead, hurt feelings fester into deep-rooted anger and bitterness. Our call is to make up for hurt feelings and seek reconciliation, whether we are the offended or the offender. Both sides are our responsibility.

Theoretically, when someone makes up, it should be forgive and forget. The reality of making up is that it props up wounded emotions, but does not strengthen them. Of course, wounded relationships have to be picked up before they can be rebuilt, but the time after a make-up is the most emotionally unstable time in a relationship. This is especially true if the problem has been deep-rooted and an ongoing source of frustration. Once two people get a problem out in the open, forgiveness and reconciliation is applied, and then there *must* be a time of rebuilding.

The beginning of reconciliation is like a truce between warring factions. Both sides are willing to make amends, but deep down there is still a sense of wariness. There may be hope, but it resides among wary feelings. Even the smallest offense can have the biggest reactions. Or should I say, overreactions? Even if we aren't consciously looking for an infraction, our emotions are. Some of the biggest blowups can come after two sides make up – especially if they live in close quarters, such as a marriage.

Perhaps our expectations are over inflated. The other person has promised to do better, and when they fall short, we not only slip back into the same feelings of frustration, but our disappointment crushes hope – if we allow it to do so. Our attitude causes us to think, *I thought they would do better, but look, they are doing it again. Nothing has changed.*

It may be that everything has changed. Recognition of a problem is the first step in making a meaningful change to behavior. Once I realize I'm doing something wrong, I know I need to start working on my negative reactions and destructive behaviors. But personalities and learned behaviors don't change in an instant. Not only do we have to reconcile, but we also have to rebuild. We rebuild ourselves and then the relationship. We must also give the other person time and encouragement to change and rebuild as well.

While we can only see the outward behavior, there is much we can't see going on inside the other person. They may be trying to stop doing a destructive behavior, failing, lamenting over their struggling efforts, and reminding themselves to change. As with my earlier testimony, I caught myself falling short in my anger, but always realized it and prayed about my failure. Outwardly, it looked like nothing was changing for quite some time. That's because no one could see when I stopped my behavior. They only saw when I failed.

Over time, my reactions became fewer, and I learned to catch myself and defuse my over-reactions. But it took time. No one but me saw my efforts. It was frustrating to be in the midst of change, but only have failure be noticed. Though my behavior changed, it was easier for others to recognize wrong, but not see the changing behavior slowly emerging.

To make matters worse, each shortcoming appears as a failure that dashes hope. That's because hope is hanging on the expectation of perfection. We naturally become hypersensitive to failure when reconciliation is made with the promise of change. Though we may be growing, don't be surprised if the other person says, "See, you always do...", or "See. You still never..."

Be encouraged to persevere, even if no one notices. Assume the best in the other person, even if you can't see immediate results. Otherwise both sides will be frustrated and give up.

Let me reiterate what has been said. Little annoyances look bigger when we hang all our expectations on perfect behavior. It's not realistic to expect someone to change in a moment. People need time, encouragement, accountability, and forgiveness. Extend grace instead of demands. Otherwise our own reactions derail the change taking place in the other person.

When we set out to rebuild a broken relationship, it lacks a secure foundation. It's like a house balanced on props. One bump and it starts collapsing again. Our natural reaction is to point at the collapse and say, "I knew nothing would change," and allow it to fall. If our frustration is bad enough, we might even be tempted to start kicking out the rest of the support beams to aid in its collapse.

The wiser choice is to stop the collapse with a word of encouragement, bear the other person up, or take positive steps to stop our hard work from collapsing. We often see reconciled marriages collapse quickly. Things may seem to be going well for a short time, but when the bump comes, each side of the marriage begins collapsing and taking down the other. The hope of change is lost when people's unrealistic expectations are dashed. It doesn't have to end this way.

Notice I said 'when a bump comes'. It will come. When we reconcile and resolve a deep-rooted conflict, the other person is going to falter. So are you. This is why we have to take the step of rebuilding seriously. Reconciling without rebuilding will not succeed. Just as a house on a weakened foundation is destined to collapse, a relationship built on a truce / reconciliation will not stand.

Working out the problem causing the stress is the first step. Now there has to be an effort to rebuild what has fallen apart. There must also be an effort to be the support for the other person. Don't passively let the effort collapse. Certainly don't aid in the collapse. Refuse to accept failure and rush to support instead of rushing to abandon.

Let's use a word picture. Suppose a homeowner discovers a termite infestation. Depending on how long the termites have been in the house, the damage could be extensive. Getting rid of the termites is the first step. The problem can't be resolved while the termites are running free and causing damage. Once you rid your house of the termites, something has to be done about the damage. If the problem was identified early, there may not be much to repair, but if there has been years of bitterness eating away at the structure, a lot of repair is in order.

Reconciling is getting the infestation out of a relationship, but it does not repair the damage. Removing what was decaying the wood doesn't resolve the problem. The damage has to be removed, and the repair has to be done.

This is what making up does in a relationship. It identifies the problem infesting the marriage, but it doesn't fix the damage. Therefore, simply making up leaves the relationship in a volatile state, and the slightest bit of stress will threaten the weakened structure.

When you see the walls beginning to collapse, intervene to stop it. Taking a sledgehammer to the problem doesn't stop a fall, it hastens it. In the same way, reacting against failure with an emotional outburst doesn't resolve the problem. The wisdom of Proverbs gives an answer, but it's one of the hardest solutions to live by. **Proverbs 15:1**

> A soft answer turns away wrath, But a harsh word stirs up anger.

The simplicity of this truth is profound in its meaning. A soft answer props up the other person – and ourselves. This is probably the hardest passage to apply to our lives for it goes against normal human nature.

As a conflict arises, what is our natural reaction? We want to meet force with force, fire with fire, an eye for an eye and a tooth for a tooth. When we hear angry words, the normal reaction is to answer with a similar tone. We entrench ourselves and prepare for battle. It is difficult to meet wrath with a soft, understanding answer. It's hard to look through the emotional outburst of another person and pick out the information and leave the destructive baggage behind. Yet this is exactly what we must do if we want to resolve conflict with rational dialogue.

We all are guilty and even as I write this, I'm reminded of how many times I've fallen short. Angry answers spark emotions and human nature rises up to meet the challenge through the flesh. But God has provided a better way. The Bible says the flesh and the Spirit are at war and cannot agree. The principle above shows the truth of this statement. My flesh does not agree with giving a soft answer, but there is no other way to see God working other than to surrender our emotions and obey His word.

The hard truth is that meeting anger with anger never resolves anything. Quite the opposite. Neither side is listening to reason, and both sides are trying to force their will on the other. It never works, but we always apply the same failing methods. The reason is our emotions are driving us instead of being tools.

As I said earlier, emotions are great servants, but they are terrible masters. When we allow emotions to race out of control, we are submitted to them and they are lords over us. Then we are taking direction from something that has no rational end in mind.

To give a soft answer requires control over my emotions and humility. I feel I deserve more respect than this person is showing me; therefore, I feel as if I have the right to return fire.

It's hard to humble ourselves because it feels like we are giving the advantages to the other person. It's as though we have allowed them to get away with a wrong – a violation against our persons. But this is just a feeling. In reality we are taking control of the situation and using the weak things to combat the mighty. This is exactly what God said He would do. He uses the weak and feeble things to overcome the strong.

Emotions are mighty and human nature is strong. They use brute force to dish out blows to the other person, or even to ourselves. Yet God uses humility to overcome the mighty emotion, and uses submission to gain control. When we submit to God's ways, miracles happen. It isn't just our efforts, but the promises of God that turn defeat into victory. It boils down to this question: Do we trust our emotions and human nature, or do we believe God and put our trust in His word?

When I use a soft answer to turn away wrath, I have said in my heart, "Lord, I trust your word and that you will work through my faith." A soft answer appears weak, but it comes from a heart that is strong in the Lord. It takes strength to push our emotions aside, but the promise is that it turns away wrath. Out of control anger doesn't have the power to defeat a soft answer. The emotional storm loses its punch when it passes over the gentle spirit.

Reconciliation is possible – and seeking to overcome anger and bitterness is a command of God. Bitter and broken relationships are a constant stress to our minds, but God has given us a plan for emotional health. As with all of God's instructions, it requires submission through faith.

Applying these things is not easy. In fact, it is impossible through human nature. Only the Spirit of the Lord can empower us to overcome our natural reactions and stand firm. Let's wrap up this chapter with the words of **Ephesians 6:13**

> Therefore take up the whole armor of God, that you
> may be able to withstand in the evil day, and
> having done all, to stand.

Notice, our role is not to overcome, but to stand. It is God's Spirit that overcomes. We prepare our hearts and put on the spiritual armor by applying God's word to our lives now, so we can have a foundation in which to stand *when* the evil day comes.

We will all be tempted and we will all have to face difficult circumstances. But the one who stands is the one who establishes their heart in the Lord and begins dethroning human nature from their own lives. Only then can we effectively deal with the behaviors of others. Self must be dealt with first. And this is much easier said than done. However, it is God who works in you to accomplish His will. He is your strength to overcome.

# Life Applications

- Memorize Proverbs 15:1
- Meditate on this passage. Think about situations that cause you to answer harshly.
- Strategize a response now. Whether you are right or wrong, plan ahead to answer with a gentle tone.
- Read Proverbs 25:15
- Work on speaking gently - even when in the midst of conflicts or disagreements.
- Read 1 Peter 3:4
- Refuse to accept your natural response of escalating in to an angry tone. Handle conflicts with a gentle spirit.
- Read Matthew 5:9
- Seek to reconcile relationships regardless of who is at fault.
- How should you handle your reactions when the other person rejects reconciliation?
- Take time to review Life Applications from previous chapters.

# Don't Let the Past Haunt You

**1 John 3:20-22**

[20] For if our heart condemns us, God is greater than our heart, and knows all things.

[21] Beloved, if our heart does not condemn us, we have confidence toward God.

[22] And whatever we ask we receive from Him, because we keep His commandments and do those things that are pleasing in His sight.

One bad choice can lead to a lifetime of regret. Sometimes the regret we feel is a string of poor decisions or a character flaw that continues to haunt us.

When we recognize our failure, it's hard not to feel guilt. But guilt is a *terrible* motivator.

Guilt tends to drive us farther from our goal of success, not toward it. When we have feelings of guilt, our natural reaction is to withdraw. It might be to withdraw from people, withdraw from the Lord, or withdraw from life. Guilt can create a fear of failure, knowing each failure will create more guilt. It can become a perpetual loop.

Guilt does not have to remain in our lives. In fact, it shouldn't be a part of the Christian life. Guilt must be dealt with by either facing our past, facing our weaknesses, or facing our irrational feelings.

God forgives, but guilt does not. When we know our feelings are irrational, we must learn to deal with them in healthy ways. This falls into the practice of taking every thought captive, which we covered previously. Once we identify guilt as an unjustified feeling, we must make the effort to cast it out of our mind.

Feelings are fickle. Sometimes there is no reason to feel badly, but our heart may still condemn us. This is not something out of the ordinary. That is why the Apostle John addressed it. There are times our heart will condemn us and the only real solution is to believe that God is greater than our heart. By faith, we cast guilt's power aside. God is greater than unstable emotions, which attempt to drive us into a fleshly-minded way of thinking.

When our heart comes back around, we find encouragement because of our confidence in God. The foundation of our confidence is that we are living a life focused on doing the things that are pleasing to God.

Our feelings of guilt may indeed be justified – at least to a point. Guilt is something the Lord has built into our emotional makeup for a purpose. As long as it serves within its intended purpose, it can be healthy. I say healthy because it's like pain. It is intended to prevent further damage, but it is not intended to be our constant companion. If it remains, this indicates something is wrong.

For the Christian, guilt should serve to reveal a problem or character flaw we are not dealing with. When we have those feelings, it is not intended to be punishment, but rather to reveal what the Lord desires to purge from us.

There is a difference between conviction and guilt. Conviction is the process of the Holy Spirit revealing something wrong. It isn't revealed to make us feel degraded, rather it is God's indication that He is about to do something positive in our heart.

Conviction is the Holy Spirit revealing something harmful and contrary to our spiritual health, or revealing something needing to change in how we relate to others. It is like a light shining in our dark hearts to reveal a hidden problem. However, when we don't deal with the problem, or if we handle conviction in an unhealthy way, it festers into guilt.

Let's go back to my own testimony. For many years I acted with selfish anger. My eyes were blind to my own faults, though I should have been able to see it. God orchestrated circumstances in life to put me into a position where I had to come face-to-face with my failure. And then the Lord convicted me. I was guilty and I knew it. But the purpose wasn't to heap guilt on my shoulders and make me miserable. It was to reveal the flaw to me so I would look to the Lord to change my life. As I quickly discovered, I was incapable of overcoming my own character flaws because they were rooted deep within my corrupted human nature.

The problem was revealed, I felt convicted by my behavior, and then I began turning to the Lord for deliverance. God revealed the flaw and convicted my heart because He was about to do something miraculous. He was about to overcome a flaw that I could never overcome – even in my best human effort.

When God reveals failure, it is so He can do the miraculous. Conviction is the evidence of what God is about to do. This is exactly what the Lord was revealing to His people in **Lamentations 3:22-26**

22 *Through* the LORD's mercies we are not consumed, Because His compassions fail not.

23 *They are* new every morning; Great *is* Your faithfulness.

24 "The LORD *is* my portion," says my soul, "Therefore I hope in Him!"

25 The LORD *is* good to those who wait for Him, To the soul *who* seeks Him.

26 *It is* good that *one* should hope and wait quietly For the salvation of the LORD.

The book of Lamentations was written by Jeremiah shortly after Babylon destroyed Israel and took the nation away as captives. Jeremiah and a few of the poorest of the people were left behind. To understand the power of this passage, we need to understand the events leading up to it.

Israel was given the Promised Land as a symbol of God's unmerited favor. At the time the nation entered the land, God said they were not receiving the promise because they were better than the nations that inhabited it before them. The nations were being driven out because of their wickedness, and if Israel became corrupt, they too would be driven out (Joshua 23:15). The Lord made it clear on several occasions that the land was His. As long as the people followed Him, they would enjoy the blessings, but if they departed from God, they couldn't take His blessings with them.

It's similar to us today. How can we expect to bask in the Lord's blessings if we are not abiding in His presence?

Israel fell after generations of moral decline. At the time before Babylon conquered them, the Lord sent Jeremiah out to witness their complete departure from God. The people were even using the Lord's temple as a worship center for pagan gods. After much pleading with the people, the Lord allowed Nebuchadnezzar to conquer the nation. Yet this happened with the promise that the Lord would preserve His people from complete annihilation, and in seventy years, the Lord would visit the remnant to bring them back again.

This takes us to the Lamentation above. Even though the people turned from the Lord, praised idols for their prosperity, offered their children as sacrifices, and cast away any semblance of morality, God showed His heart was still clinging to the people. Judgment was actually a call of repentance, and the Lord was even showing mercy in the face of judgment. The purpose was not to destroy the people. It was to drive out the iniquity that was destroying the people.

In the midst of lamentation, a promise shined. Compassion was still renewed every morning, and those who sought the Lord and waited on His deliverance would find goodness. If this is true for a nation mourning over their devastation, how much more true is this for our era, where Jesus is our High Priest and advocate? In any circumstance of life, the Lord's desire is for our good.

Even when we are experiencing consequences for our foolish choices, the Lord is in the midst of the hardship with renewal, mercy, and a call to seek Him – with the promise that we will find His goodness.

When we make bad choices, we may indeed suffer harsh consequences. Though our lives may be temporarily covered by shame, fear, and sorrow, the promise remains that the Lord is good to those who seek Him and hope in His salvation.

This promise was given to those who were in rebellion against the Lord. It was written for the benefit of those who were suffering the consequences of their actions. Though the Lord didn't promise to remove the consequences, He did promise to work through their difficulties and reveal good to those who turned to His faithfulness.

You and I will suffer consequences for many bad choices. Most will be minor, but some may be severe. Even in the depth of our remorse, we have the promise of a new day, filled with mercy and hope. And all we must do is turn, seek the Lord, and put our hope in His salvation. If we do these things we may still suffer, but we'll emerge from the other side into joy and confidence in the Lord. Those who hope in Him will have hope in their life – regardless of anything they have done beforehand.

To those who hope in God's mercies, consequences are never eternal.

The passage above was written for people suffering for their sin. Those who turn their hearts back to the Lord had this promise of assurance. On the other side of grief stood comfort, hope, and the blessings flowing from the goodness of the Lord.

This is what God is doing in your life. Have you made mistakes you regret? Made a foolish choice? Are you struggling through consequences? Welcome to the human family. Repentance doesn't exempt us from consequences, but it does turn our hearts to the Lord. Even if there is a hard road ahead, we can now look forward with hope.

One thing promised is that though consequences may judge us, the Lord's mercies are always new. We then can look to Him for salvation and press ahead with hope. It becomes an opportunity for the Lord to remove the flaw from our character, change our hearts, call us to seek the right way, and then wait in quiet peace for His salvation.

Problems can seem threatening, but when we step back and look at it from the eternal perspective, it's easier to endure. It's not easier because the problem disappears, but because we know the Lord will bring us out of the valley as a changed person. Even the most shameful mistakes can become trophies of grace.

Remember, we are not perfect in our daily lives. We are pressing toward perfection.

# Don't allow people to chain you to the past

Our lives change, but perceptions of our character in the eyes of others sometimes does not. A man or woman of understanding will rejoice with us and encourage us as we are transformed by God's Spirit. However, there are people who will try to bind you to your past. Do not allow someone to drag your past along and throw it back into your life. Some refuse to accept change. These people are blind to their own need for mercy and want to deny God's grace to those who they deem as unworthy.

Some have compared it to crabs in a bucket. When a group of crabs are piled into a bucket, they won't allow one another to escape. If one starts making progress, other crabs will pull on them until they lose their grip and fall back into the pile. Human nature often does this to others.

Sadly, during the times you need encouragement the most, people will come along, dragging the chains of your past, and declaring your failure. This is when we stop and encourage ourselves in the Lord. The Bible calls Satan our accuser, and he not only uses guilt as a weapon against us, but he also uses people who are fleshly minded. Even spiritually professing people can be flesh driven.

Night and day he accuses us before God and man.[61] The Lord doesn't listen to your accusers. Once forgiven, He promises to put our sins as far from us as the east is from the west.

This promise paints a beautiful picture. East and west can never meet. North and south do. If you go north, you will eventually reach the North Pole and begin heading south. But there is no East Pole. Or West Pole. If you go west, you go west forever. Going east is a never ending journey. For this reason, we can have confidence that when our past is in the past, the Lord will never follow us around and cast it at us as an example of failure.

Unlike people, the Lord doesn't call up our past and tie it into our current struggles. Once sin is forgiven, it's buried forever.

If guilt rises up, it is not God reminding you of the past. The Lord will never say, "Remember when you did this?" The Bible says our sins are cast into the depths of the sea of God's forgetfulness.[62] It's not that God can't remember, but it's the scripture's way of saying God will never bring up your past once you have been forgiven. It is blotted off the record.

The Bible often uses the word 'blot' to refer to forgiveness. Sin is a wrong that must be accounted for. In Revelation, the books are open and all the world is judged, but something interesting happens to those who are forgiven. Jesus Christ has paid the debt. One of His last declarations came on the cross when He cried out, "It is finished." Something is lost in translation, for Jesus used the word, 'Tetelestai'. It's a Greek word used in accounting which means, "Paid in Full." It was used when the debt owed had been paid and the account is taken off the record. Any who are in Christ are under the payment of the cross.

---

[61] Revelation 12:10
[62] Micah 7:19, Hebrews 8:12, Hebrews 10:17

Our debt is paid, the account is blotted out, and our transgressions are taken out of the way. Our record may be filled with blots, but who can accuse someone of a blotted out record? When the books are opened, those who are forgiven may have had an ugly past, but it is no longer visible on the record. Some of us have a lot of blots, but who can accuse us before God when the record has been purged?

Satan may keep records, but his testimony is worthless. People may keep records, but according to Jesus, any who hold their companions accountable are actually judging themselves – not those whom they are accusing.[63]

The records of wrong I keep means nothing to God. Whether I'm remembering my own guilt, or the wrongs done to me, my record book only serves as a burden on my back. It has no value and its contents are useless. His books are the only ones that matter.

Those contrary to God do not understand grace and will not easily accept the Lord's work in our lives. Even though it may be unintentional, people can become pawns in Satan's attempt to discourage us and drag us back into the past. This is even true among our families and churches.

People who have been wounded are especially vulnerable to holding on to the past. Just as we must go through the process of forgiveness as we discussed earlier, those we may have wounded will struggle if they don't forgive. Forgiveness frees the wounded as well as the one who did the wounding. And it opens our hearts to receive the salvation of the Lord.

Salvation is not only referring to our hope of heaven. It is also saving us from the hardships of life. I'm not only saved from hell, but I'm saved from bitterness, guilt, anger, and any other thing that robs me of the peace of God. We are also saved from bitter consequences.

Turning from my ways to the Lord may not remove consequences, but it does change the fruit of consequences.

---

[63] Matthew 18:23-35

Instead of my ways leading to destruction, the Lord takes over the reins and guides us to His goodness. What would have destroyed our lives will now emerge into the promise that all things work to the good of those who love God and are called according to His purposes.

Our situation may still be painful, but beyond the pain is hope for those who have turned from their own ways and now wait on the Lord. Consider some extreme examples. Someone who commits murder will still be tried and convicted. They still face punishment by our legal system.

Repenting doesn't turn back the clock and undo the crime. Yet when God becomes Lord of this person's life, they now face the uncertainty and the consequences of their actions with new hope. On the other side, they will emerge into the plan of God. While others may enter the same circumstances with hopelessness, the believer can face it with hope.

Our harmful actions may come back on us, but the Lord now uses it to grow us, prune us, refine us, and transform our lives. Hope. Never does the one who trusts in the Lord face life without hope.

I used an extreme example, but it applies to every avenue of our lives. Whether it be a small deed or big one, consequences follow our pattern of behavior. While the Lord doesn't honor those who temporarily turn to Him to escape consequences, the Lord does honor those who turn to Him to change their lives.

When others uphold our past to declare our shame, we who trust in the Lord will emerge from failure with renewed lives. We can then uphold our past as a testimony of God's mercies, and instead of shame, our failures become trophies of His grace.

# Life Applications

- Memorize Lamentations 3:22-26.
- Practice dealing with guilt in healthy ways.
- Do you struggle with feelings of guilt? Explore your guilt and identify the cause.
- Read Colossians 2:14.
- Apply God's principles to your guilt:
  - Repent (or turn) from the behavior.
  - Trust in God's forgiveness through Christ.
  - Ask forgiveness from anyone you have wronged.
  - Trust your wrong to Christ. Declare it nailed to the cross.
  - Bring thoughts and feelings captive to the obedience of Christ. Expel them from ruling your life.
  - If feelings of guilt remain, believe the promise that God is greater than your heart.
  - Obey the command to be thankful and rejoice.
  - Once the problem has been dealt with, turn from it and focus on truth.
  - When feelings arise, cast them down and turn again to rejoicing, thanksgiving, and trusting the Lord.
- If someone brings up your past, use it as a testimony of God's grace.
- Review Life Applications from previous chapters.

# The Deception of Assumptions

**Luke 6:37**
> Judge not, and you shall not be judged. Condemn not, and you shall not be condemned. Forgive, and you will be forgiven.

The Bible says much on the subject of judging. At times we are instructed to judge certain things; other times we are warned not to make ourselves judges. Most of the time when we are instructed to judge, it is in regards to resolving conflict, evaluating what claims to be truth against the scriptures, and evaluating ourselves against the standard of Christ. God does not allow us to judge the hearts of others.

At the heart of assumptions is this one glaring word – judging. When we assume the intent of someone's heart, we are placing ourselves in God's role, assuming we can discern the hidden thoughts of someone else's heart, and then we condemn their intentions. In reality, we are condemning the thoughts of our own heart, which we have assumed, and forced into the motivation behind someone's words or behavior. Our assumptions we are forcing upon others is actually our own judging attitudes.

Back in my school days I had two classes with two girls who were once friends. One mentioned to me that the other girl wasn't speaking to her. "I don't know why she's mad at me," she said.

In the next class the other girl said, "I wasn't mad at Susie until she walked by without saying a word. She used to be my friend, but now she doesn't talk to me." Neither would speak to the other but both assumed the other was angry.

Each person was upset – not because of anything that was said or done – but because they each assumed the other had ill feelings toward them. They went from friends to enemies because they filled the silence between them with assumptions born out of their own hearts. Though it was something conjured up in their own hearts, the assumption was the standard by which each judged the other.

The majority of our conflicts are based upon judgmental assumptions. She did this because she just thinks _blank_. Fill in the gap. He just did that because he is trying to annoy me.

Sadly, the assumption we apply to our perception is almost always wrong. Let me reiterate this. Almost *always* our assumptions are wrong, yet we treat them as if they are facts.

Like most people, you have probably had others accuse you of acting with an intention that never even entered your mind. So have I. I've had people get angry because of an assumption that did not exist. In fact, many times when being told of my ill intentions, I'm caught off guard. I wasn't annoyed, angry, or frustrated. But now I am – because the natural response to an accusation is to get defensive. Then a conflict is born where none previously existed.

I also have been guilty of this very thing. We all have this flaw. But an amazing thing happens when we start assuming the best in others instead of the worst. Rather than being offended or suspicious when something isn't clear, we begin to see those around us in a positive light. Working relationships flow smoother, we become less defensive, and we handle daily issues in a more positive way. It makes for a happier life. Even conflicts resolve with less tension. Assuming good instead of bad changes our entire attitude.

It's easy to assume ill intentions where none exists. This is a deception and temptation designed by the enemy to cause discord. When our spouse does something that bothers us, we see a sinister motive behind the action and it stirs our anger all the more. How many arguments could be avoided if we assume the other has good intentions instead of evil.

Once we realize this erroneous way of thinking, we can guard our attitudes, and avoid the deception of negative assumptions.

The truth is, when someone annoys us, they probably don't even realize their actions are bothering us. Annoyances are petty, but when assumptions enter the equation, it inflates annoyances into a greater problem. Little annoyances become breaches in our relationships. Things that are small and should be shrugged off are inflated into giant conflicts, not because the offense was great, but because we assume the intention was evil. The intention we assume becomes the focus rather than the actual problem.

This happens to everyone who works or lives in close relationships – school, church, work, and especially the home. The closer we are to someone, the more likely we are to adopt assumptions. What's worse is the longer we project our assumptions on someone, the more resentment grows. People end up angry and bitter at each other, and neither side can point to a specific incident as the cause of conflict.

The more I assume you have ill intentions toward me, the more I resent your behavior – and I interpret every action as affirmation of my assumption.

Negative assumptions also create negative feelings in the other person because they become defensive and pick up the bad vibes we are sending out. A negative attitude projects in our demeanor.

Assumptions are one of the problems God's command to not judge helps us to avoid. You and I have no way to see inside someone's heart. We cannot discern the hidden thoughts and intents of the heart. When we set ourselves up as the judge of someone else's motives, we have fallen outside of God's design. God will allow us to judge ourselves for our judgment. He will not judge the other person for our perceived wrong.

When our negative feelings are projected onto someone else, we are then judging others for what is in our own heart

– not what is in theirs. And by our judgment, we are condemning ourselves, for we are acknowledging the wrongs we have conjured up.

We must consciously determine not to judge the hidden intentions of others, or assume someone has a negative attitude in their heart. It is your responsibility and my responsibility to stop and reevaluate our assumptions. It is our responsibility to stop ourselves from saying, "That person is just doing this because..."

The Christian walk is meant to express the love of God He has poured into our hearts to those around us.[64] If we are truly viewing the world through the eyes of God's love, we should be assuming the best instead of the worst.

Many conflicts can be avoided if we stop our minds from responding to temptation. Instead of thinking others are out for our harm, we should start assuming they are out for our good. Let innocence be the assumption until proven otherwise. If we assume the best we will see the best. If we assume the worst, we will only have eyes to see the worst. And we'll bring out the worst from others. The real problem is that we are adopting our perspective from the flesh instead of from the Spirit.

There is another truth to consider. If we show people our expectations, they will often live up to those expectations – whether good or bad. Let me give an example.

When I was younger, I worked in a warehouse. In that job I witnessed two opposite examples of management. Steve was the manager of our branch and he was always positive. When someone was hired, Steve would come back to check up on the new hire. He would say something like, "Paul is doing a great job, isn't he?" Steve always asked about someone or something with the assumption of a good outcome.

---

[64] Romans 5:5

His attitude did two things. It immediately put others in the frame of mind to look at the new hire from a positive perspective. Instead of thinking about what Paul could have done that was a mistake, we looked for his successes. Unless there was a serious problem, the answer was always, "Yes. He's catching on and working hard."

The second benefit to Steve's attitude came from Paul. When Paul heard that Steve thought he was doing a good job, Paul stepped up his game to meet this expectation. He immediately had a positive attitude toward his own contributions and he was motivated to rise higher. We had a great working environment, great teamwork, and a productive branch because everyone drew encouragement from the manager's positive assumptions.

Steve was promoted to a corporate position and a new manager took his place. We'll call him Mr. J. Mr. J. was the polar opposite of Steve. He took the assumption that someone was failing and assumed the worst until proven otherwise. When he checked up on Paul, he said something like, "Do you think Paul is going to work out?" Or, "If Paul is screwing up, let's not waist our money on him."

Even if Mr. J. had a less condemning way of asking, the perception would still be negative. Which would have a more positive response? "Is Paul doing okay?" Or, "Paul is doing a good job, isn't he?"

On the first question, the initial impulse is to think about Paul and try to remember if he fell short in any way. The second question would only have a negative answer if Paul was really failing. While the negatively phrased question stirred doubt and scrutiny, the result of a positive question created a positive expectation.

People were on edge around Mr. J. Morale plummeted, people pointed fingers at one another when a problem arose, production went down, and people left the company. Mr. J. expected people to fail and people began living up to that expectation. One of my co-workers said, "I'm just tired of this. Why bother if no one in management recognizes my work?"

Two assumptions. Two reactions. When people live under a positive assumption, they are motivated to excel. When people are put under the burden of failure, or required to prove they are not failing, it taxes the relationship and nothing thrives. The only difference between these two men was that one assumed the best from people, and the other assumed the worst. Both got out of the relationship what they assumed to be true.

Oftentimes, when we have negative assumptions about people, it's a sign that something needs to change in our own heart. A thief doesn't trust others because he assumes everyone thinks as he does. So he assumes they are untrustworthy. An unfaithful spouse assumes their counterpart is unfaithful because that's what is in his or her own heart. People shouldn't have to prove they aren't wrongdoers. People should have to prove they are failing before we have a reason to doubt them. Even then, we have to allow them to change.

The above example is also true with negative attitudes. If I have a negative pattern of thinking, I will assume you are thinking negatively, too. Because I have a bad attitude, I assume your mistake is spiteful because you also have a bad attitude. Even if this is not true, it becomes reality in my mind because it's the way I think. And if I begin accusing you of having a negative attitude, what happens? The accusation stirs up negative feelings and creates a defensive attitude that can grow into a bad attitude. Unless you take healthy steps to avoid it, you will be pushed into the assumption I have placed over you.

It's my responsibility to shape my own attitude so I am not adopting what has been projected onto me by others. It is also my responsibility to not assume the worst in others and avoid projecting negative feelings on them. I must not project attitudes they may not have had and may have never thought of until being accused.

Remember our earlier discussion where someone accused me of spewing venom from the pulpit? They quoted me as saying something I never thought. They were so adamant that I listened to the recorded message to see if I had said these things. Not one of the hateful quotes I supposedly said were ever spoken.

How can someone hear words that were never spoken? It's this dangerous tool of temptation – negative assumptions. The message addressed something God was convicting them of doing, but they assumed I was targeting them. Since this person assumed I was thinking negatively, this is what they heard.

Though the words were never said, they interpreted them according to the negative assumptions they were sure I meant. It was an attitude born in their own heart, but their assumption projected it onto others. This was also why they were having other conflicts in the church.

This is what you and I are tempted to do on a daily basis, so we must be careful. When I assume you are thinking negative things toward me, I interpret your words, actions, facial expressions, and tone of voice according to what is in my own heart. You may have never even felt what I'm assuming you feel, but to me, it becomes an assault.

I can even assume you have a conniving attitude that does little things for the sole purpose of irritating me. I then have attributed my imaginations to you, and even if you're completely innocent, you are guilty in my judgmental heart. You've been accused, tried, and convicted in my mind, even if nothing I believe is based on reality. Perceived wrongs can appear just as real as an intentional offense.

Have you unwittingly fallen into this mind-set?

Some will read this and say, "That's paranoia." True, but to varying degrees, we are all guilty. Some people have obvious problems with paranoia, but if we're honest, we are all in this boat to some degree.

Emails are a great example of misconceptions. Since tone of voice can't be written, the reader applies the tone and will always react according to their own perception. If you've been in a corporate environment, you have likely seen conflicts based on a misperceived tone of an email.

Good humor can sound like an insult, and an honest question can appear to be sarcasm. The next time you find yourself saying or thinking, they are doing this with ill intent, you have become the judge of someone's heart. And your assumption can never be a judgment based on righteousness.

It is your choice. When someone irritates or annoys you, the voice of assumption will rise in your heart and tempt you to be the judge of that person's heart and intentions. Consider this passage from **Romans 2:1**

> Therefore you are inexcusable, O man, whoever you are who judge, for in whatever you judge another you condemn yourself; for you who judge practice the same things.

Intentionally or unintentionally, you will irritate others. Are you thinking of little ways to annoy the other person? If so, something needs to change in your heart, but most of the time the answer is, 'No'. You make mistakes. Should you be accused of an evil heart because you inadvertently annoyed someone? If the answer is no, then you have no right to impose that standard upon other people.

When you make a mistake, is it an intentional conspiracy, born out of a bad attitude for the other person? If no, then you have no right to stand in judgment of the other person. If the answer is yes, then you still have no right to judge the other person. For our attitudes do not belong to others. What I may be thinking has nothing to do with the heart of the other person.

The solution is to stop ourselves each time we catch this thought. Assume others are unaware that their actions bother us. Communicate without accusation. Assume mistakes are just that. I'll reiterate this again. Most people are unaware that what they have said or done is an offense to us. They cannot see our feelings, so we must not assume they are targeting our feelings.

We *must* reject the negative assumption that arises from the flesh, and instead assume the best in others. Assume our spouses really care about us. Assume our coworkers are trying to do their best. Assume our church members are doing as we are, struggling to live out this Christian life the best way we can, while living in bodies that are corrupted by the flesh. Just as we do, our church family fails. Sometimes they fail big. Sometimes we fail big. We want grace for ourselves, and we should extend this grace to others.

Assume each person is trying to live out the words of Jesus found in **John 13:35**

> "By this all will know you are My disciples, if you have love for one another."

The true evidence we are disciples of Christ is our love for one another. Assume those around you are struggling to live this command out, and that they need your help to do so. Just as you need their help. Warring among ourselves can never fulfill the unity of the church, and most wars among people are founded upon a misconceived assumption.

Most marriages begin breaking down because of misconceived assumptions.

Assume the best in others, and strive to help them live out the best. In doing so, you will find your own attitudes will change and relationships will begin to grow. Assume your negative attitude is wrong. Assume others have a positive attitude, and begin adopting this attitude for yourself.

When wronged, it is possible to communicate without accusation. But when our assumptions are the driving force, bitter conflict is inevitable.

Assumptions are a tool of deception. But as the Apostle Paul said, "We are not ignorant of his (Satan's) devices." Having this knowledge is the first step. Now you must adopt the godly perspective on a daily basis.

Assume the best in others. Expect the best out of others. Try to bring out the best in others. When they fail, treat others the way you expect to be treated when you fail.

# Life Applications

- Memorize Luke 6:37.
- Let's do an exercise. Think about the statement, "You're a real friend, aren't you?"
- Assume this was sarcasm.
- Now assume this was said by someone showing appreciation for your help.
- Does the same statement stir different feelings based on the perception you applied?
- Think about the people you interact with. Spend time adopting a positive perception for each person. Assume they appreciate your feelings.
- Actively apply a positive assumption to each interaction you have from now on – even with those you count as enemies.
- Commit to expecting the best from others.
- When you catch yourself assuming negatively, bring that thought captive and force yourself to assume positively.
- Plan how you will respond today, so you will have the right mind-set when needed.
- Take time to review Life Applications from previous chapters.

# Living Out These Truths

When you try to live by these principles, there will be times you'll fall short. The temptation is to give up, but you must make this a lifelong effort. God has promised His greatest rewards to those who overcome. Overcoming does not mean we just make a one-time change. Sometimes we must wrestle against our weaknesses. It can be a slow transition from harmful habits and behaviors to healthy ones.

One day you will feel successful, then someone will do or say something that will stir up negative feelings. You'll slip right back into your old ways of acting and it will discourage you. That's okay. We all struggle with the same problem. Stop trying to accomplish godly principles through the flesh. The Bible says that we are changed into Christ's likeness as we behold His glory. Focus on your relationship with Christ and rest in grace. Then take grace and share it with others.

Overcomers are not those who are invincible, but those who get knocked down, brush off, and get back up again. An overcomer is someone who refuses to let the flesh remain in control of their lives. It's not falling down that defeats the person. Not getting back up is what causes defeat.

You will blow it, and when you do, don't toss your hands up and say, "I tried." Refocus your eyes on what is eternal, change your perspective to walking in the Spirit, and begin again. Every day is a new challenge, but also a new start.

Unforgiveness and self-centered fixations are two of the great robbers of joy. Unforgiveness quickly festers into anger and bitterness. These strip our minds of peace and strain our relationships to the breaking point.

Becoming fixated on ourselves also festers into many internal struggles. When I'm focused on myself to the point where I'm evaluating right and wrong based on how things cater to my will, the world always appears out of balance.

Let's explain the idea of 'self' more clearly. When it comes to correcting behavior, we must focus on ourselves first. Until my behavior is in order, I can never have the right perspective to discern what is happening in the actions of those around me. I must remove the plank out of my own eye first, and then I can see clearly to deal with the specks in those around me.

When it comes to relating to people and the world around me, I must not look at myself first. This is what I mean by not becoming fixated on self. If I am judging motives, fairness, and other things based on my own desires and preferences, I'll have a self-centered perspective and will be unhappy unless the world revolves around me.

We must learn to judge (or evaluate) our own behaviors and attitudes first when it comes to correcting behavior. We must also learn to put others first when seeking good. Have you met someone who demanded their way in every situation? Someone who was a taker and only gave when there was something to gain? Are they ever happy? Maybe for a moment, but this happiness is dependent on getting their way the next time something comes up. And this will be the first person to complain that not getting their way is unfair.

God's design is for you to put others ahead of your own interest. This is hard to live by, but it is the only way to fully experience love in our relationships. A relationship of takers is each person playing tug-of-war with the other, for each is trying to satisfy themselves. Then no one is satisfied and both sides feel deprived. But a relationship of givers satisfies both parties, and above what was expected. Consider these passages.

**1 Corinthians 10:24**
Let no one seek his own, but each one the other's *well-being.*

**1 Corinthians 13:4-7**
4 Love suffers long *and* is kind; love does not envy;

love does not parade itself, is not puffed up;

⁵ does not behave rudely, does not seek its own, is not provoked, thinks no evil;

⁶ does not rejoice in iniquity, but rejoices in the truth;

⁷ bears all things, believes all things, hopes all things, endures all things.

The one who seeks the well-being of others will experience love. Love doesn't seek its own. By its very nature, love gives. It has to be outward focused in order to be love. Love begins with God. He pours love into our hearts by the Spirit and then calls us to give what He has provided. And we can give love because the Bible promises it will return to us in time. We are not in control of love, but we do have the promise of faith which says, "Give and it will be given, pressed down, and overflowing." It may not even be from the person we expect it from, but God will fulfill His promise.

It's as Ecclesiastes 11:1 says, "Cast your bread upon the waters. For after many days it will return to you." Most people never experience the increase of love because they are not willing to wait for it to return. The Lord is the increaser of our blessings, and He will test your faithfulness. God will give you both the opportunity to wait for His promise, and the opportunity to turn back and miss the promise.

It's ironic that self-focused attitudes never fulfill, but those who are outward focused find joy in life. It's as the scripture states in **Proverbs 11:24-25**

²⁴ There is *one* who scatters, yet increases more; And there is *one* who withholds more than is right, But it *leads* to poverty.

²⁵ The generous soul will be made rich, And he who waters will also be watered himself.

When life is valued based on getting what I want or ordering my world in specific ways before I can be happy, soundness of mind will elude me and fulfillment will be absent.

God has designed life so we are fulfilled through loving Him and giving to others, not by serving ourselves. The Bible also says the eyes of man are never satisfied. If gaining my way is the focus, I am the person who withholds more than is right, but never seems to be fulfilled. This is why many people are in emotional poverty. They are holding on to more than is right, but instead of abundance, their satisfaction shrinks away into nothing. It is the giver that God promises to satisfy.

Our goal should be to become a blessing to others, and trust in the Lord to fulfill us. He will do so through those around us, through the peace in our hearts, and by the blessings He personally brings into our lives through opportunities and His power.

It's the generous soul that becomes rich – not the hoarder. Generosity does not only mean money. It means to give to others through our lives. It means seeking the good of another over ourselves. It means trusting in the Lord's promise that if we scatter our desires by sharing our lives with others, He will increase us with abundant satisfaction.

We can hoard love just as we can hoard possessions. Grappling for my way simply does not work. I've never met a happy selfish person, but I have met many happy givers.

As we have seen, the Christian must live under the instruction, "Let no one seek his own, but each one the other's well-being." This is at the heart of the love God has given us. Love does not seek its own. So our attitudes reveal whether or not we are walking in love. The Lord said, "My ways are higher than your ways." Human reasoning operates contrary to God, but God designed us and knows how to give us soundness of mind, peace, joy, and all things of value.

The flesh demands that we grapple for the gusto of life because we'll be deprived if we don't get our gratification before someone else takes what we want. The truth is that God is our exceedingly great reward, and He knows how to satisfy. In fact, God is the only one who can truly satisfy.

Unforgiveness stirs anger because we are not getting something we feel we deserve. Sometimes unforgiveness is born out of a wrong done to us, but it doesn't change the fact that we must cultivate a forgiving heart. Someone once said bitterness is a poison we drink in hopes the other person will be harmed.

Bitterness truly is a poison to our soul, and as long as it abides, peace cannot take root.

Let's go back and review our foundational passage from **2 Timothy 1:7**

For God has not given us a spirit of fear, but of power and of love and of a sound mind.

This is God's design. The Lord never intended for emotions to be our masters. Fear, frustration, unhealthy desires, and any other harm that springs from our flesh may challenge our minds, but God has given us the plan of victory.

Remember our discussion of the first murderer, Cain? He was angry with his brother out of jealousy – not by anything his brother did to him. The flesh began rising up and attempted to take control of Cain's mind, but the Lord warned him that he should rule over sin and not be ruled by it. Whether it is selfishness, or the spirit of fear, we have the instructions of the word that teaches us how to walk in the Spirit and overcome.

Fear is not a sin any more than the selfish desires that stirred Cain's mind. It wasn't the temptation that was sinful. It was Cain surrendering to temptation and allowing it to rule him. The same is true for any temptation. Doubt isn't a sin, but unbelief is. Unbelief is when we disbelieve

God because we now trust in doubt. Anger isn't a sin, but outbursts of wrath and vindictive behavior is. Fear isn't a sin, but surrendering our mind to fear is, for when we do so, we can no longer believe God, and the Bible says, "Whatever is not of faith is sin."

Faith is believing God and putting our trust in Him. Faith comes when God reveals His truth to us and His plan to our hearts. We then must trust in the Lord, or put our trust in something else. None of these are sins until we submit our minds to the flesh.

One thing is certain; today's victory will not be tomorrows triumph. It can help build the foundation for tomorrow, but tomorrow you will have to renew your mind, die to the flesh, and stand firm on the truth.

The Bible says, "To him who thinks he stands, take heed, or else he will fall." Never quit pressing ahead. Never sit on your past accomplishments. Never grovel in your past failures. Each day is new, and don't be discouraged if you blow it.

The Bible says a wise man falls, but gets up again. It does not say the wise don't fall, but that they don't wallow in defeat. They are wise because they recognize that in the end, victory is a promise from God. But the promise is to those who obey. Part of obedience is forging ahead where God is leading – even if the way is difficult.

Though you may feel defeated, press on. Even if your emotions seem uncontrollable, press on. It is not the short-term, but the life-long goal that becomes our promise to overcome. Always keep this in mind; the Bible says God sees the end from the beginning. That means He isn't measuring your success based on who you are, but who you will be when you stand before Him completed in Christ.

Scripture promises, "He who began a good work in you is faithful to complete it." God won't drag you toward victory. He leads. You must follow. Even if you don't feel like battling on, keep pressing toward the high calling of God. If you're tired, He is your strength. If you're weary, He promises to renew you like an eagle. If you fall, you have the promise of **Psalm 37:23-24**

23 The steps of a *good* man are ordered by the LORD,
And He delights in his way.
24 Though he fall, he shall not be utterly cast down;
For the LORD upholds *him with* His hand.

Once again, this is the word 'man' in the general sense, so the promise applies to all. If you fall, what sustains you? The Lord, for He upholds you with His hand. God is able to make you stand,[65] but God will not force you to follow Him.

The times when you need to heed the counsel of God the most is also the time when you will not feel like applying it. When you're angry, frustrated, fearful, or tempted, your flesh will attempt to take the reins of your heart. It is far too easy to let go and be carried by the emotions rooted in the flesh. It is during those times when we have to deny ourselves, put off the desires of the flesh, and walk in obedience. God's ways indeed work, but it can't work if we refuse His word when we need it most.

Let me again reiterate an important truth. You will blow it. Don't beat yourself up, but regroup, submit yourself to the Lord, and press on. It is the Lord who upholds you; therefore, your only concern is to get your feet back under you. You've already been picked up, so don't hang there in defeat.

In this book I have shared many things about myself few people have known until now. I have a compulsive personality. Sometimes this can be a benefit, but most times it's something that attempts to rule me. My angry outbursts had its roots in compulsive desires. There are other areas where I also had to overcome compulsiveness. Most people would be surprised to find out about this side of me. For that I am grateful to the Lord, for He has led me out of many unhealthy ways of thinking.

---

[65] Romans 14:4

This is what God desires for each of us. The Lord wants you to experience His goodness and victory over the flesh. He is your strength to overcome. When battling a behavior, it can seem impossible to overcome, but over time it loses its grip. Even so, our past ways of thinking can rise up and attempt to regain control.

I still have those compulsive feelings at times. My family has no idea I am a compulsive. For the most part, I don't think about it either. For a brief moment, those feelings will arise on occasions, and I have a moment of decision where I cast them away. For example, in the car my kids are often laughing in the backseat. I'm a person who enjoys quiet. Their noise often stirs those feelings, but I realize it is a selfish attitude. Should my kids be scolded because I want silence? Instead, I picture the pleasure of their laughter, and cast down my desire to bring them under the control of my whims. It's this way with many things.

While my flesh has its compulsions, these urges have no power to rule over me unless I surrender my mind to them. I know if I try to control the world around me to satisfy selfish emotions, it will make me and those around me miserable. This is the types of causes that creates stress.

Do I still blow it? More times than I'd like to admit. I find myself wrestling with unhealthy feelings and desires. Sometimes they get the best of me, but even then, God is merciful. He rescues me, sets me on the rock of Christ, and I begin again.

A compulsion is a desire which tries to align the world with our whims. And when someone or something can't be controlled, frustration builds. This is why we must stop and evaluate ourselves the moment those feelings begin.

There is no frustration when the feeling is evaluated and rejected as something of no value. As the habit of evaluation takes hold, the decision is a brief moment. The things that once seemed insurmountable are now a split second evaluation and decision. Then they are gone. And forgotten. No pressure. No bottling up anger. It's realizing it has no value – and often negative value, so it is cast away as rubbish.

I share all of this for a reason. If you battle these things, it's important to understand you are not unusual. And you are not less spiritual because of this. Every person has internal battles – even those who appear to be pictures of peace and perfection. They are battling their own wars in the flesh in ways you cannot see. This is also why we have no right to condemn those who fail. Though someone may fail in areas we don't see as a temptation, we also fall short in areas they are not tempted.

God does not reject you because of your failures. In truth, the breech between us and God is our rejection of Him as He calls us to let go of our flesh and walk with Him in the Spirit.

Sometimes we reject God because we love the flesh. Other times we run from God because we feel unworthy, due to a weakness of the flesh. Both end up becoming a barrier between the Lord and us.

Acts 20:28 says God purchased our redemption with His own blood. This shows God's goal is not to punish our failures. He died to rescue us from failure. He didn't die in vain, but the cross is the evidence that God will go to the ends of the earth to rescue you from the things that bind you.

True shame is when we don't believe God. He took on our debt, died for our sins, and then declared that He is the Good Shepherd who seeks every person who goes astray. To then not believe He loves us and not recognize His desire to restore us when we fall is to disbelieve the love He has already shown – and continues to show each time He pursues and reconciles us to Himself.

The greatest barrier to the sound mind is the whims of the flesh. That is where fear, doubt, lust, and every negative feeling is born. It's God's pleasure to pull you out of the miry pit and set your feet on the Rock of Christ – His salvation.

Having a sound mind is not within your power. It's a promise of the power of God on your behalf. Let's conclude with a review of this amazing passage in **Philippians 4:6-9**

6 Be anxious for nothing, but in everything by prayer and supplication, with thanksgiving, let your requests be made known to God;

7 and the peace of God, which surpasses all understanding, will guard your hearts and minds through Christ Jesus.

8 Finally, brethren, whatever things are true, whatever things *are* noble, whatever things *are* just, whatever things *are* pure, whatever things *are* lovely, whatever things *are* of good report, if *there is* any virtue and if *there is* anything praiseworthy -- meditate on these things.

9 The things which you learned and received and heard and saw in me, these do, and the God of peace will be with you.

Do these things and the God of peace will be with you. It is God who guards our hearts and minds. This is a command with a promise. Do these things and you will find true peace. This is where the sound mind has its foundation. May the God of peace be with you!

If you found this book to be helpful, please rate it on Amazon.com or other retailers. Share this with others who also may need encouragement.

If you would like more information about living a Spirit filled life and what it means to walk by faith, I'd like to invite you to read *The Victorious Christian Life*. You can email me through my website at http://www.eddiesnipes.com or at http://www.exchangedlife.com.

# Life Applications

- Memorize Proverbs 11:24-25.
- Pray for God to make this passage part of your life. Pray for the faith to believe God will make your soul rich with His goodness.
- Give to others as an act of faith - believing God's promises.
- Think about ways you can give of yourself to others.
- Plan now as to how you'll respond to situations where you would normally expect your way. How will you put others first?
- When you feel you have failed, evaluate yourself and plan how you'll respond next time in a godly way.
- Encourage yourself in the Lord, believing He upholds you and is calling you to stand.
- Take the Life Applications for each chapter, put them on notecards, and review them throughout each week. Discipline yourself so they don't slip from your focus.
- Be thankful, for God is with you.


You may enjoy these other titles by Eddie Snipes.
*The Victorious Christian Life*. Living in grace and walking in the Spirit
*Simple Faith*: How every person can experience intimacy with God.
*I Called Him Dancer*. Christian fiction.

*Please take time to rate this book on Amazon.*

Connect with the author at eddiesnipes.com.

# Acknowledgments

My first acknowledgment is to the Lord. He has allowed me to experience many hardships and successes that were necessary in order to understand the things in this book.

A special thanks goes out to my parents, Linda and George Snipes. I had the privilege of being raised in a Christian home and we continue to have a close relationship.

To my grandmother, Lucille Morrow. She recently celebrated her 89th birthday. She is also the one who led me to the Lord where my life became new.

To my wife Jennie and my kids, Emily, Lucy, Natalie, Sophia, and Abigail. Yes, all five of my children are girls! I am proud of each of them.

To my wife's parents, Arch and Mary Nelson. Your encouragement over the years has been appreciated. I'm grateful to have such wonderful in-laws. I couldn't ask for a better family.

The Christian Authors Guild. I have served as president for the last two years, and it's an organization that has been a great source of encouragement to me.

I'd also like to thank my former manager that I used as an example in this book. It is said that only a handful of people shape our lives and mentor our character. Through hardships under this working relationship, I grew into a deeper understanding that I could have never found any other way. I am grateful for our paths crossing and I often pray God will reveal Himself to you. His blessings await, and may He open your eyes to see it.

I'd like to give a special thanks to Tony Edge. Your fellowship and counsel has been an encouragement to me. It's rare to find someone who can listen to ideas and discuss controversial topics, and debate from differing perspectives without worrying about offending. Your gentle spirit is refreshing.

I'd like to give acknowledgment to Richard Wilkins. Your humble spirit and heart for the Lord is an inspiration. I've enjoyed our friendship and fellowship over the years.